The Teachings of Freemasonry

by H. L. Haywood

Edited by Michael R. Poll

The Teachings of Freemasonry

A Cornerstone Book
Published by Cornerstone Book Publishers
An Imprint of Michael Poll Publishing

Cornerstone Book Publishers
New Orleans, LA

First Cornerstone Edition - 2008
Second Cornerstone Edition - 2013

www.cornerstonepublishers.com

ISBN: 1613421516
ISBN-13: 978-1-61342-151-2

MADE IN THE USA

Table of Contents

The Teachings of Freemasonry

PART I
INTRODUCTION

WHAT is this all about? This is a question I asked myself many times during my initiation experiences. It is a question, brother, which you doubtless asked yourself, and so has every other man who has forged on to the end of the Third degree. The language of the ritual, stately and beautiful as it usually is, is to most of us a mystifying speech; and the stations and stages of the dramatic actions are equally bewildering to the novice. Therefore is it that we ask the question, "What is it all about?"

After we have become familiarized with the ritual, and have learned something of its drift and its meaning, we discover that the Fraternity itself, as a whole, and apart from any mystery in any one part or detail, is something almost too complex to grasp. A member grows so accustomed to the goings on of his home lodge, that he loses his first sense of strangeness, but even so he hears ever and anon such things of the antiquity, the universality, and the profundity of Freemasonry as it exists in history and in the great world, as to make him feel that for all his familiarity with one Masonic lodge he is very much in the dark about the Masonic Fraternity in its entirety.

What is Freemasonry? What is it trying to do? How did it come to be? What are its central and permanent teachings? It is to answer these questions - and they are such questions as visit the mind of almost every Mason, however indifferent he may be - that the philosophy of Masonry exists. To learn "what it is all about," in the whole more especially than in the part, it is for this that we philosophize about our mysteries.

"How would you answer the newly-initiated brother who asks the question, "What is this all about?" Did you ask yourself that question? How did you answer it? What advantage is there in trying to learn what Freemasonry means in the largest sense? What is meant by "the philosophy of Masonry"?

Why do we philosophize about it? How many reasons can you give for the necessity of philosophizing about it? Have you ever read a book explaining Freemasonry?"

The individual who secures membership in a Masonic lodge becomes thereby the heir to a rich tradition; that to which initiation gives him access is not something put together in a day, and it will profit him little if he makes no attempt to enter into his patrimony. He must learn something of the history of Masonry; of its achievements in the great nations; of its outstanding teachers, and what they have taught, of its ideas, principles, spirit. Initiation alone does not confer this knowledge (and could not): the man must himself strive to make his own the inexhaustible riches of the Order. He must be taught the larger purposes of the Fraternity to which he belongs.

There is no authorized interpretation of Freemasonry. The newly initiated brother does not find waiting for him a ready-made Masonic creed, or a ready-made explanation of the ritual - he must think Masonry out for himself. But to think Masonry out for one's self is no easy task. It requires that one can see it in its own large perspectives; that one knows the main outlines of its history; that one knows it as it actually is, and what it is doing; and that one knows it as it has been understood by its own authentic interpreters and prophets. It is not easy to do this without guidance and help, and it is to give this guidance and help that such studies exist as this new series on which we are now embarking.

"What is the reason for the study of the teachings of Freemasonry? How much of Freemasonry can a man learn from initiation? How else can he learn? What would you give as "the larger purposes of the Fraternity"?

"Why should one try to think Masonry out? Could you, unaided by books or another person, write an intelligent and intelligible answer to the question, "What is the meaning of Masonry?"-

There is still another reason for a study of philosophy, or as we here more familiarly describe it the teachings of Masonry. Our Fraternity is a world-wide organization with Grand Lodges in every State and practically every, Nation. In this country alone it is a vast affair of millions of members and many separate and independent Grand Lodges. To sustain and manage and foster such a society costs the world untold sums of money and human effort. How can Masonry justify its existence? What does it do to repay the world for its own cost? In one form or another these questions are asked of almost every member, and every member should be ready to give a true and adequate answer. But to give such an answer requires that he shall have grasped the large principles and be familiar with the outlines of the achievements of the Craft, and this again is one of the purposes of our philosophizing on Masonry.

How can we arrive at a philosophy of Masonry? How are we to learn the authentic interpretation of the teachings of Masonry? What is the method of procedure whereby one who is neither a general scholar nor a Masonic specialist may gain some such comprehensive understanding of Masonry as has been called for in the preceding paragraphs? In short, how may a man "get at it?"

One way to "get at it" is to read one or two good Masonic histories. There is no need to go into detail or to read up on the various side issues of merely antiquarian interest; that is for the professional student. There is only need to get the general drift of the story and to catch the outstanding events. To learn what Masonry has actually accomplished in the world is to gain an insight into its purposes and principles, for, like every other organization, it has revealed its spirit through its actions. From a knowledge of what the Order has been and what it has done in the past one can easily comprehend its own present nature and principles, for Masonry has never had a need to break with its own past! The Masonry of today does not make war on the Masonry of yesterday. Its character emerges clearly from its own history as a mountain stands out above a fog; and what it has ever been - at least in a large way - it is now, and doubtless always will be.

This same history forges ceaselessly on evermore renewing and making itself. It is going on today and the process is one that keeps publishing itself to the seeing eye, for, after all, there is not much that is secret about the rich and tireless life of the Fraternity: indeed, this life is constantly revealing itself everywhere. Grand Lodges publish their Proceedings; men engaged in the active duties of Masonic offices make reports of their functionings; students of the Craft write articles and publish books; Masonic orators deliver countless speeches; special Masonic conferences, whatever be their nature, make known their business; most of the more important events get into the daily papers; there are scores and scores of Masonic papers, bulletins and journals, weekly, monthly and bi-monthly, and there are many libraries, study clubs and learned societies everywhere endeavoring with tireless zeal to make clear to members and profane "what it is all about." So it turns out that to learn this for one's self one does not need to take any one man's word for it; he can look about, and listen, and read up a little, and thereby form his own conclusions. It is amazing, when one looks into it how much of the labor going on in the Craft is designed to make clear, and to propagate and enforce the principles and teachings and spirit of our great Order. To learn what are these teachings asks of us no rare talents, no "inside knowledge," but only a little effort, a little time.

What would be your estimate of the monetary cost of Freemasonry to the United States? to the world? How many Masons are there in the United States? in the world? How many lodges are there in the United States? What does Masonry give in return for its cost?

How many Masonic histories can you name? Whose is generally considered the best? What advantage does a Mason derive from reading such a history? Would a knowledge of Freemasonry's own past be of any help to a lodge worker in present day affairs and problems? What is the character of Freemasonry as it "emerges from its own history"? What is there secret about the Order? If a man were to ask, How can I find out what is going on in American Freemasonry? how would you answer him? Can you name half a dozen Masonic periodicals? Have you ever read the Proceedings of your own Grand Lodge? How many can you name of the "few great ideas" about which Masonry constantly revolves? What is the difference between an "idea" and an "ideal"? How can a member learn what are these "great ideas"?

Where and how are they taught? Did your initiation cause you to think about life differently?

To the novice the Masonic world seems very confusing, it is so many-sided, so far-flung, so clamorous with voices and the din of action; but this, after all, need not frighten us away from an attempt to grasp that world with a comprehensive understanding, for all of Masonry constantly revolves about a few great ideas. These ideas confront one at every turn - what becomes more familiar to an active Mason than such words as "Brotherhood," "Equality," "Toleration," etc., etc. - so that the youngest Entered Apprentice need have no difficulty in getting at them. If he does get at them, and if he learns to understand them as Masons understand them, they will help him greatly to gain that comprehensive and inclusive understanding which we have been calling the philosophy of Masonry.

Nothing has been said as yet of the great teachers of Freemasonry.

In the older days there were Anderson, Oliver, Preston, Hutchinson, etc.; then came the philosophers of the middle years, Pike, Krause, Mackey, Drummond, Parvin, Gould; Speth, and others, and in our own day Waite, Pound, Newton, etc, etc. In the writings of these men the great and simple ideas of Freemasonry become luminous and intelligible, so that he who runs may read.

In addition to all this the member may take advantage of those interpretative devices which are a part of the Craft itself, the lectures and monitorial explanations built into the ritual of all the rites and degrees. None of these are infallible - nor are any of them made compulsory to believe but even when they stray farthest from the original meaning of our symbols they are always valuable in reviewing the ideas and ideals of multitudes who have originated or used them.

Thus much to show why we should strive to make for our own mind a philosophy of Masonry, and in how many ways one may arrive at that philosophy. There remains only one word in caution. A study of the philosophy of Masonry is not a study of Philosophy; the Masonic student as such may have little interest in Plato and Aristotle, in Neo-Platonism, Mysticism, Scholasticism, Rationalism, Idealism,

Pragmatism, Naturalism, etc. Masonry touches upon the circumference of each of these and the other major philosophical systems, no doubt, but there is no such thing as a Masonic philosophy any more than there is such a thing as a Masonic religion. We speak of a philosophy of Masonry in the sense that we speak of a philosophy of government, or industry, or art, or science. We mean that one studies Masonry in the same large, informed inclusive and critical way in which a political economist studies government or an astronomer studies the stars. It would be a blessed thing if more of our members were to lift up their eyes from the immediate and often petty affairs of their own lodge room in order to gaze more often on those profound and wise principles which are to our Fraternity what the laws of nature are the universe.

Can you name a great Masonic teacher not mentioned in section? Whom do you consider the greatest interpreter of Masonry? Can you tell the differences between the groups mentioned? What is idea at the bottom of present-day Masonic thinking? In way does the ritual explain itself? What is a "philosophy"? What does the word mean? What means the phrase, "A Philosophy of Freemasonry"?

PART II
THE MASONIC CONCEPTION OF HUMAN NATURE

IF A MAN wishes to develop a swift race horse he must first understand much about the nature of horses; if he would build a powerful engine he must needs understand something of mechanics; if he would build a house he must have at least a working knowledge of building materials, of proportion, of stresses and strains, and what not. Similarly, he who undertakes to work with men must, unless he wishes to invite certain failure, understand something of human nature, which is to say, what kind of a being man is, what can be done with him, what one may hope from him. It is safe to say that the largest number of attempts to reform and improve man fail because of ignorance concerning human nature.

The science which deals with human nature, which asks what man is, how he came to be, what his destiny is, is known as Anthropology.

There is such a thing as a Masonic Anthropology, or Science of man. Masonry deals with men: it is trying to do certain things with men, to shape them in a certain way, by certain means. Unless Masonry understands the nature of men, and is able to deal successfully with that nature, it will as surely fail as the man fails who tries to operate a farm without any knowledge of agriculture.

What kind of a being is man, as Masonry understands him? It is quite impossible to give any adequate answer to this question inside the limits of so brief a work as this. It is quite impossible even barely to mention all of the most elementary features of such an answer. We are compelled to deal in generalities, and very briefly at that.

We may say, first of all, that to Masonry man is a being that can be educated. This is implied in the Masonic ritual from end to end, and it is taken for granted in every phase of Masonic teachings. The candidate comes in the dark, ignorant, a child, needing to be led about by a guide, and cared for by patent guardians. At the end of initiation he stands on his own feet, he sees the light, he has in him a new vision, a new nature. Under the veil of symbolism the novice is presented as a shapeless stone, or Rough Ashlar, fresh from the quarry. When the "work" is done he is a Perfect Ashlar, a stone hewn and finished, ready for its place in the wall. If this can happen to a man inside the lodge from it can happen outside; if a man can be born again under Masonic influences, he can also be born again under other equally powerful influences. To Masonry man is not a static being: he is educable, and by educable is meant, not that every man can be given a school training, but that man, by his nature, is capable of growth, of improvement, of development.

How would you define "anthropology"? How would you go about the scientific study of human nature? What would such a study include? Of what value is it to us in our every day life? Why do we have a "Masonic Anthropology"? How would you answer the question, What does Masonry teach concerning the nature of man?

This view of human nature is optimistic, and it is therefore unfortunate that all cannot hold it. But such is the case, for there are many who cling to some form of fatalism about man. These may not believe that man's life is fixed by the stars, as the astrologers once believed, but it amounts to the same thing. They may believe that before man was created God preordained all the details of his life; or they may with certain scientists, hold that man's life is wholly shaped by environment; or they may think that accident or luck shapes all. In any event these persons hold that man is a being helpless to change himself: if he is strong he can never become weak; if he is weak he can never become strong. Man is a static being, of a fixed and unchangeable nature; what he is, that he had to be, and will ever remain.

To the Mason this is a cardinal error. He is under no illusions about human nature. He knows how weak we all are; how much viciousness remains in the most saintly nature; how ignorant the average human being is and will always remain. He knows how often man is his own worst enemy; how the generality prefer to be governed by others rather than themselves. Knowing all this, a wise Mason will not expect the impossible but he will expect that under the pleadings of a right influence most men will respond, and he believes that we should do all we can to improve human life even though we can never make it perfect, or even satisfactory. More than that, a Mason believes that on the whole the being progresses, and that in the long hereafter of the being's life men and women will reach levels of development now unattainable. Human nature, as hinted forth by all the devices of "progress symbolism" scattered through the three degrees, is not static, stationary, fixed in its present form, like a cast of iron.

Nor does Masonry teach that human nature is a depraved thing, like the ruin of a once proud building. Many think that man was once a perfect being but that through some unimaginable moral catastrophe he became corrupt unto the last moral fiber of his being, so that, without some kind of supernatural or miraculous help from outside him, he can never of himself do, or say, or think, or be aught but that which is deformed, vile, hideous. Those who hold to this kind of anthropology usually claim to know how supernatural help may be brought to bear on that corruption which is human nature, and they usually believe themselves to be of the party which controls that help, and they also usually believe that only those who accept supernatural intervention according to their own formula have any hope whatever of escaping from the original sin into which every man is born.

Do you believe that a man's nature can be permanently changed for good or ill; or do you believe that what a man is when he is born that he will ever remain? What is fatalism? How many different forms of the theory of fatalism can you recall? Do you believe that a man must remain the helpless victim of heredity, luck, environment, etc.?

An individual Mason here and there may hold this "depravity view" of human nature: that the Order not hold it or countenance it, is abundantly proven by the ritual, and by all our Masonic principles. Masonry bases on the organization and control of those very forces in human society which are most natural: charity, association, mutual help, and all the thousand moral influences which play ceaselessly about the human being. It is time that the lesson in the Third degree is the lesson of regeneration: the candidate comes as one whose old self must die, in order that a new self may be born; but this new life into which the candidate is born is not in any sense supernatural.

Do you believe that the human race progresses? What is progress? Do you believe in the doctrine that man's nature is from birth a depraved and corrupted thing? Where did this theory originate? How would you convince a man that Masonry does not hold to the "depravity view" of human nature?

What is the relation of Masonic teaching to the theory of Evolution? Can the philosophy of the ritual be made to harmonize with the theory of Darwin? Here is a question with which Masonic thinkers of our day are everywhere confronted, and it is a question difficult to answer. Answered it must be, however, in some sense, for Evolution gives us a new and distinct and challenging conception of human nature. Man, as "Darwin pictured him, is not the same being as that conceived in the mind of St. Paul, or Jean Jacque Rosseau.

It is impossible for us here to grapple with this vast question, but there is one phase of it too important for our purpose to be passed over. According to some of the theories of Evolution "man is not man as yet." He is only a part-being, a creature in process, with a nature unfinished and doomed therefore to wait for fullness of life in some remote future. The present writer believes that there is not one iota of word or act in the whole ritual of the Order to agree with such a reading of human nature. To Masonry human nature is far from complete and anything but perfect, nevertheless it is man as he is now endowed who will strive for progress and perfection. With the faculties he now possesses, with the five senses, with his hands and his head, with such endowment as each is now equipped he must build his Temple, or unfinished will it ever remain. To consider man as in a mere state of flux; to picture him as a jelly-like being always to assume new shapes - this is to depart from all sound thinking. Man, in the essential structure of his being, is now all that he can ever be. He will never have wings like a bird, he will never possess fins and gills, to live in the water: in all eternity he can have but two eyes, and two ears, and two hands. He will be divided by sex into male and female; he will be born into social relations, and he will evermore live in the midst of what we call external nature. These are fixed and absolute realities and any thinking which plays fast and loose with these realities is no thinking at all. To learn what are the fixed facts of our nature; to learn how human society and the external world necessarily behave, and to adjust one's self accordingly, so that one may live in harmony with the way things really are, that is wisdom.

What is evolution? Who first discovered the theory? Who was Charles Darwin? Do you believe in evolution? Does Masonry ?

We live in certain fixed relations. God is, and we are bound to him in a thousand ways. Nature is omni-present, and to live is to live in relationship with her. Always there are other human beings about us, and always will there be. To live in harmony with God, man and nature, is happiness. It is wisdom. It is mastership. The Master-man, the Master Mason, is not one who has been granted a few secrets in some miserable occultism as some vainly believe and teach; he is one who has so mastered and organized the fixed and universal facts and conditions of normal human life that he is happy in his living. He could not be happy in his every day life if he believed his nature itself to be corrupt. He has too much common sense to believe that in this world all is as it should be. He sees no reason for postponing life until he has somehow evolved into super-manhood. He takes life and the world as he finds them, and does the best he can with them.

Man is not an angel. He is not a perfect being whose faults are always due to an unfriendly environment, nor is he a debased, rotted creature, wallowing in mire until touched by the arbitrary grace of some supernatural power. Nor is his nature in a state of flux, so that he may be human now, and something other than human after millions of years. We can not learn what man is by the long roundabout of some abstract theory. We must take him as he is. He can not be taught much, but he can be taught. He is incapable of receiving much light but he is able to use his intellect a little. He can never be an ideal friend or brother but he is always capable of some brotherhood. He has plenty of selfishness, cupidity, lust, ignorance in him; but he has a lot of nobility in him for all that. Only a sentimentalist will abandon his part in the uplift of man merely because that enterprise always fails. Because a mature Mason has the commonsense view of human nature he will never expect too much of the world by way of charity, brotherhood, enlightenment and the like, but even so he will toil faithfully all his days to those great ends, knowing that human nature is capable of great things.

In what sense is man's nature now fixed and completed? What is "wisdom"? How can a man learn to be happy? How would you define the "commonsense" view of human nature ? do you believe in it? do you believe that Masonry teaches that?

PART III
THE IDEA OF TRUTH IN FREEMASONRY

A CANDIDATE enters the Masonic lodge room in thick darkness. There is no light within him, and there is none about him. His progress from station to station is in quest of illumination; he passes from degree to degree seeking more light: when at last the scales fall from his eyes, and the illumination comes, the whole lodge greets the climax with a battery of exclamation. The sun, the moon and the stars move through the symbolism of the three degrees as they pass through the houses of the sky. References to daybreak and dusk, to midnight and to the meridian day, are omnipresent throughout the ritual. Learned men debate with each other concerning the origins of this element in our symbolism, many believe it has descended to us from the Light Religions of the ancient world, be that as it may, all Masons understand that light is nothing other than the symbol of truth and knowledge, and the prevalence of that symbolism is an indication of the importance to be attached to truth and knowledge in any study of the greater teachings of the Fraternity.

Can you remember any "light symbolisms" not mentioned in the above? Why do you suppose, did ancient man worship the sun, moon, and stars? Can you find any traces of this early worship in the Bible? Why did "light" come to be taken as the symbol of Truth?

William Preston, to whom the Craft is so much indebted, and who largely shaped the Second degree as we now have it, believed it to be the chief end of Masonry to instill wisdom and convey knowledge. Under his hand the lodge became a school room; the Master, a teacher; the candidate, a pupil. In more or less orderly fashion a whole system of learning was set forth, ranging from the five senses to the fine arts, and it was made abundantly clear that no man can remain a genuine Mason who holds truth lightly or chooses to remain in ignorance. The liar and the ignoramus may somehow get into Masonry, but no Masonry can get into them.

There is a difference between "truth" and "knowledge," it goes without saying, and that difference is not often lost to sight by the ritual, but on the whole our system uses the two words interchangeably. Truth is sought for the sake of life. We human beings are set in the midst of a world every element of which is ceaselessly influencing us. Nature is not an inert background, but a system of positive forces; the sun warms us; the rain falls on us; our existence is bound up with natural processes. Other human beings impinge upon us, their lives interacting with ours. In our own selves, in our mind, body, emotions, volitions, forces are tirelessly at play. A human being cannot stand immovable and uninfluenced in the midst of life as a rock stands in the wash of the tide. His life goes on every moment influencing and being influenced. And life is full and rich, happiness comes, when we so understand ourselves, and the world, and the forces of nature, that we harmoniously adjust ourselves thereto. The report of what nature, the world, life really are, that is truth; and the items of information which we need to have in order to know the truth, that is knowledge. A wise man desires truth and seeks knowledge, not in order to pose as a scholar or a learned man, but in order that he may live happily.

What was William Preston's conception of the lodge? Was there a public school system in England in his day? What is the difference between "truth" and "knowledge?" How would you define "truth?" Do we seek "truth" for "truth's" sake or for "life's"? What is the connection between truth and happiness?

How a man finds knowledge is a matter of comparative indifference; he may learn from books, or he may never read a page; he may attend school or not; he may gain information by himself or from a master. That is for the man's own choosing, and Masonry offers no recipe for an education. But enlightenment is a thing every Mason stands pledged to seek, and seek it he must if he is to be a Mason in fact as well as in name.

Do you believe that it is a Masonic duty to seek knowledge? Why? Are you seeking knowledge? How? What effect would it have on your lodge if all its members were well educated men? Would it make for the unity, harmony, and therefore the happiness of its members? Can you think of a legitimate excuse for ignorance? If Booker T. Washington, too nondescript even to know his own name or birthday, could earn a splendid education while working in a coal mine, couldn't every man do as much, barring ill health?

From the point of view of Masonry, ignorance is a Sin. Usually a man excuses himself for his ignorance by saying, "I had no opportunities. I have had to work since a child. I could not go to school." This self-justification is a fallacy all through, not only because many men have won a schooling in spite of poverty, but because one may gain an education without going to school at all. We have night schools, free public libraries, daily papers, magazines, cheap books, and countless agencies which fairly beg men to learn. Moreover, if a man is not content to remain in ignorance, he can always learn from experience, observation, and from his work. Considering how ample are the opportunities to learn knowledge and truth, there is no excuse for ignorance, and the only reason for it is that a man is too lazy, or prefers darkness to light. Usually it is his indolence that is to blame. Ignorance is sin.

I recently asked of the manager of a considerable business enterprise, "From which do you suffer the most, the dishonesty of your employees, or their general ignorance, indifference, stupidity?" "What we suffer from their dishonesty," he replied, "is as nothing from what we lose by their lack of knowing how to work, and knowing this business. Deliver me from the ignorance of the majority of men. Business suffers a thousand times more from stupidity than from dishonesty!" The whole world suffers from men's ignorance. Children grow up diseased and unhappy because mothers and fathers undertook a family without learning anything about the right care of children. The same children leave school with half-taught minds because so few school teachers understand teaching. They embark in business and found families of their own through which to perpetuate their own lack of knowledge, and thus does the world go on. Ignorance is a sin because of the unhappiness it causes inhuman life. It is a good thing for a great institution like the church to wage its war on viciousness and deliberate wrong. It is equally a good thing for a great institution like our Fraternity to make war on that mental darkness which breeds quite as much evil in the world as the corruptions of conscience.

Do you believe that "ignorance is a sin"? What does our ritual teach concerning this? In what way is it a sin? Would the politicians of the world be able to deceive the masses so easily if those masses knew more about history and about the world as it now is? In what way would widespread knowledge make for human peace?

Truth must be sought for. It is not an entity lying outside us, like a boulder on the path, but a living and changing thing, which must evermore be possessed anew, a fact which is so hauntingly bodied forth in our legend of the Lost Word, and our search therefor. And each man must win it for himself, such is the law, for it is not a commodity which can be handed by one man to another, though there are countless ways in which we can help each other to find the light. The institution which supposes itself to have discovered all truth, and to have it neatly organized into a creed, which may be received from it secondhand, as one may receive a legacy, is an institution that is deceiving itself and its followers. No institution has captured the whole truth; none ever can. No man can come into possession of the light by signing his name to a creed. Masonry has no creed. For each one of us men the truth is as a word that is lost, and each of us must himself go in search for it.

When Charles Darwin called our attention to a whole set of new facts about the development of living beings hosts of men turned on the great naturalist with revellings. They had already made up their minds about the origin of life. They were hoodwinked by their own theories. The man who makes up his mind about a thing before he has learned sufficient about that thing is a man that wears a blindfold and cannot see the truth. To be open minded; to be willing both to learn and unlearn; to be glad to revise one's old theories in order to conform to newly learned facts; and not to be afraid to depart from the crowd on its beaten path if the light leads in new directions - all this is necessary if one is to be a truthseeker, and it is all suggested to us by the symbol of the hoodwink.

A man must free himself if he is to find light; also must be glad and willing that others be equally free. If I must have a free mind then, by token of the same requirements, my neighbor must have a free mind, and I shall be glad to give him the rights of a free mind, unless I am a fool and a bigot. This is toleration. Toleration does not mean that one idea is as good as another, or that one truth is as important as another. Neither does it mean (this should be thrice underscored) that one is indifferent to all ideas or theories as though it matters not what men believe. When toleration lapses into a mere indifference it becomes a vicious thing. The real meaning of toleration is, when a man goes in search of his Lost Word, let him choose his own path, and place no obstacles therein.

But it has a greater meaning than that. The greater truths are always too vast to be won by a single mind; always must a group of thinkers work together in a close corporation. Toleration means that every such group be left free in its endeavors. It is just here that one finds the church's most frequent crimes of intolerance. When Vesaluis and his Renaissance contemporaries were working to discover the facts about the human body the church hampered them and thwarted them at every turn. The same thing happened to the geographers who explored and mapped the earth; to Newton and his colleagues who built up the science of physics; to DesCartes and his contemporaries in philosophy; to Paracelsus and his successors in medicine, and to Charles Darwin and the group of nineteenth century biologists of whom he was chief. The same thing is happening today to the group of sociologists who are trying to learn the truth about the structure of human society. It is bad enough when some individual is forbidden to think for himself, but it is far worse, it looms up as a crime against mankind, when mankind's own best thinkers, scientists, inventors, investigators, are prevented from carrying out in action that work from which alone we can learn the truth about ourselves and the world.

Mankind can never discover the whole of truth. Always and always it opens before us, like an ever-receding goal; and evermore must we continue to seek it, even as the Masonic candidate, helped in such ways as is possible, and amid many obstacles, gradually through the darkness makes his "progress" from station to station, from degree to degree, seeking light, and more light, and that mystic Word which is truth itself.

How is truth found? How do you know a thing to be true? What does the ritual teach about the nature of truth? What does the hoodwink suggest about the reasons for man not finding the truth? What is meant by a "prejudice"? How does it prevent our finding the truth? What is toleration?

PART IV
THE MASONIC CONCEPTION OF EDUCATION

THERE were no schools when Freemasonry came into existence. Medieval Europe had much learning but no great public institutions for the diffusing of it. There were a few seminaries where men might receive an "education" for the priesthood, and there were, here and there, a few monasteries, nunneries, brotherhoods, lay organizations, and what not which dispensed to a handful of young people the rudiments of knowledge. Of schools as they now exist, and have existed for two or three hundred years, there were none. Nor was there in any community a daily press, or weekly periodicals, or a library, or cheap books, or a learned society, or a correspondence school.

Before you begin a discussion of the subject endeavor to define your own conception of "education." Could you tell how youths were educated five hundred years ago? What was a nunnery? A monastery? A lay brotherhood? A seminary? When did printing first bring knowledge into the reach of the poorest ?

But there was such a thing as education, often of a high type, and sometimes of a degree never afterwards excelled for the Medievalists gave us the greatest architecture that has ever been known, and some of the greatest pictures, and much wonderful sculpture, not to mention the flowering out of the religious spirit: these gifts could not come from an ignorant and debased people, such as the medievalists are by many often supposed to have been. To erect a St. Mark's or a St. Peter's, to build such a city as Venice, or to paint such pictures as those of Tintoretto, or to conceive the ideal and spirit of the Franciscan Movement required a trained intelligence, a directed and fruitful genius, which can only come from that discipline of the human nature that we know as "education."

If the people had no schools whence came such an education? The answer to this question is found in the system of apprenticeship which was in universal use with those guilds and brotherhoods that built Venice, and erected the cathedrals, and painted the pictures, and created the sculptures. Instead of going into a public school the youth went into a guild. Instead of studying from a teacher who sits behind a desk with a book in his hand, the medieval student learned from a master in the very operations of work. Instead of receiving a diploma on sheepskin he was given the means of proving to anybody that he was himself a master workman, entitled to receive a master's wages wherever he might go.

Put yourself into the place of some medieval architect entrusted with work on one of the huge cathedrals which became at once the wonder and despair of all subsequent builders. You had to have skilled workmen. You were compelled to find men who knew how to hew stone properly out of a quarry, how to dress it in the rough, how to read plans, how to solve geometrical problems, how to carve, to erect scaffoldings, to round an arch, throw up a spire, and also, in many cases, how to organize and direct other workmen. Where would you find such men? You would draw from the ranks of intelligent youths such as gave promise of skill and you would very carefully have them trained in all these processes, and, because many of these processes were valuable trade secrets, you would take great care to bind these youths to you in a secrecy from which knowledge might not escape clandestinely to the outside world.

The necessity for educating youths into the extremely difficult arts of fine building was one of the causes which led to the founding of Freemasonry. Because of this necessity the trade union grew into a lodge. Members were bound together by solemn ties, and local organizations were compelled to affiliate themselves together into a wide Brotherhood of workmen.

The student was called an "apprentice," or "learner," for such does the word mean in nearly all languages. There were no books wherewith to teach him, so his masters taught him by means of the work itself, and the tools and practices used in the work. And since these students had to live together in closest unity it was necessary also to train them in morality, for without morality there can be no permanent association. And because these young men were to work on religious buildings being erected by religious organizations it was inevitable that religion should come to have a central place in the scheme of education. In all this we have the beginnings and the conditions out of which Freemasonry arose.

When Operative Masonry reached that stage in its history wherein it became transformed gradually into Speculative, or Symbolical Masonry, learning, or knowledge, or enlightenment (one may use any of these terms), had come to be at the core of it. But since the knowledge of actual building arts was no longer of any purpose to the members of the Fraternity the old "work" was gradually transformed into symbols and allegory, and the "apprentice" in the new order of things was set to learn the art of building manhood and brotherhood.

In the early eighteenth century when the old Operative Craft was made over into the Symbolical institution as we now know it, it happened that one of the major prophets of the new day, William Preston, was burning with an enthusiasm for education. There were schools in England for the sons of a few rich, but no school for the masses, and among those young men who found their way into the transformed Masonry there were few with any education at all. Preston said, "Let us then make the lodge into a school room. While we are making Masons of these youths let us at the same time give them the rudiments of knowledge." So he worked out an elaborate system of lectures in which were set forth something of all the subjects between the five senses and the fine arts. The Second degree as it now stands is to a great extent the result abiding memorial of that noble endeavor. When Freemasonry first came into existence in the form recognized as such by us it was very largely an educational institution. When it found its great rebirth in England during the Grand Lodge era it rapidly became a center of knowledge. It has searched for "light" from the beginning; it has always inculcated in its devotees a desire for "more light" - today it continues to hold up as its ideal of human perfection the man of "enlightenment." Therefore this emphasis which to we place on the need for light is not a hatched-pseudo-emphasis, but a passion deeply rooted in very nature of our Order, and inseparable from it.

What does the Second degree mean to you? What can you tell about Preston? Could you now improve the Second degree? how? How could the modern lodge be made into another type of school?

What is true of Masonry's attitude toward education, is equally true of its attitude toward that institution which is the custodian of education, the public school. Those who wonder why we should keep so watchful an eye upon every educational enterprise any time satisfy their wonder by a careful study the birth, the growth, and the culmination of our Fraternity.

It would be quite useless, to many another essayist has learned to his sorrow, to attempt to fashion a definition of education, for it is one of those fundamental profound conceptions which defy analysis and escape words: but even so it is a thing that we recognize without understanding it and describe without defining. There was a time when by "education" men referred to a fixed body of knowledge, inherited from past times, crowned by tradition and approved by authority, which was gotten into the minds of students by a certain fixed method. This quantum of knowledge was supposed be invariably suited to all minds, whatever their cast or bent, and the boy who could not master it was thereby catalogued among the dunces, or the lazy sorts. There was a great deal more truth in that old conception of education than the present day reformers are willing to admit but even so it is a conception which we must abandon. There is no such thing as a quantum knowledge the acquirement of which constitutes education, for education, so the psychologists have made us see, is quite another kind of thing.

A human being comes into this world quite helpless and quite ignorant. He is so dependent on others that the word "baby" is almost synonymous with the word "helplessness." He cannot talk, or read, or walk, work, or feed, or clothe himself - a being more abjectly helpless it would be hard to imagine. An adult man, if he be normal in all ways, must be able to work so well that the world will pay him money for it. He must be able to make his wants felt, his thoughts known, and his qualities appreciated. He has a wife to cherish, a family to support, a home to maintain. He must know something of the functions of citizenship. He must be able to take his place with his fellows in all those activities of normal life.

Do you know what Masonry has done toward upholding our American school system? What agencies are at work to tear down that system?

It is education that bridges over the wide gulf between the helplessness of the babe and the manifold richness of the adult nature. Parents, insofar as they are tutors of their own children, schools, books, teachers, and the individual's own experience, are all so many instruments of education, and it matters little how a man secures education so long as he is an adult able to fulfill all his normal functions in the various relationships of life. What particular kinds of knowledge a man must have, whether it be Latin and Greek, literature, science, philosophy, civics, what not, depends on the nature of any particular man and upon the conditions under which he has to live his life. Anything is good education that enables us to be happy in our life environment.

From this it will be seen that education is by its own inherent nature a social thing. It is something that prepares a man to live with his fellows, to work with them and for them, to understand them, to get on well with them. It is a thing that makes possible the fulfillment of the fragrant saying to the effect that it is a good and beautiful thing for brethren to dwell together in unity. And since education is by its nature a social thing, a thing fraught with all the fates of society, then it is perfectly self-evident that education must be defined and managed by society itself, and for society's own good. To permit any group to turn education into an anti-social engine, so that it functions against all in the favor of a few, is as foolish a thing as to turn loose upon society all the hordes of confusion, anarchy, and war.

It is because of this fact that Freemasonry is so keenly interested in and concerned for "the education of all the children of all the people." The "Temple" which the Craft is building is nothing other than the human family living happily together. The equality and democracy for which it has ever stood is nothing other than its preaching of the fact that men and women are by nature brethren and should live together as such. If there are any educational agencies, or any types of education, upon which Freemasonry wages a tireless war, it is because those agencies are promulgating an education which teaches men that we are not all brethren, and that it is not wise for us all to try to live together in harmony. Any institution which insists upon democracy as Freemasonry insists upon it must everlastingly be concerned much with the institutions of education. Like schools, like people.

An institution which demands so high an educational ideal on the part of the outside world should, so it would seem, itself set a shining example. This is the whole pith and contention of serious Masonic research societies. There is no known way whereby, through a kind of magic, we can find light in Masonry. If a man wishes to learn something of history, he studies it; so, if a man would learn Freemasonry he must study it. Initiation is no magic process whereby, without the exercises of his own faculties, and minus the necessary acquisitions of knowledge, a man may be conducted into the full glow of truth, Masonic or otherwise. Those who would become real Masons must work to that end - the light does not come miraculously but at the end of a toilsome way. There is a vast deal -far, far more than most men dream - of knowledge and truth hidden away in our traditions, our history, our customs, our laws, and, above all, in our incomparable ritual, but a man can no more become possessed of that treasure without working for it, than he can come into an understanding of Greek without studying it. Masonic Research does not mean a delving into the dust bins of antiquity for rare lore - it means a digging out of Masonry that which there is now in it for truth, and for light.

These sentences may sound like broad generalizations, but if so, they are generalizations of facts that are real enough. To some of us it seems a sin and a shame that hundreds of lodges do not scruple to push a man from one degree to another until he has had them all, and all the badges that go with them, without so much as an effort made to tell him what it all means, without so much as a step taken toward leading him into a realization of all that he has experienced. No wonder that there are so many Masons who have nothing of Masonry save the name!

Do you agree with the definition of education given in this work? Do you believe yourself to be an educated man? What has education to do with democracy? Why is there a vital relationship between the principles of Masonry and the principle of public education? How can Freemasons set a good example to the outside world?

PART V
RITUALISM AND SYMBOLISM

REPETITION is of the essence of ritualism; and since nothing can sooner grow stale or inept than repetition we find many persons who think of ritual as meaningless stage play. To go through the same performance over and over, to say the same words in the same way, and often not even to know the meaning of these actions and these words, is not that rather childish? This question, we take it, has come home to numberless Masons, especially American Masons, for in this country we have so prized originality, novelty, and individuality that we all have a tendency to despise and to fear ceremonial. It may be well for us to reflect a little on ritual, what it is, what it does for us, and why we may all, individualistic as we may be, frankly and intelligently uphold it as having a just right to a major place in the functionings of a Masonic lodge.

Do you grow weary of seeing and hearing the ritual? If so, why? Do you believe it would add to your interest in Masonry to have no two meetings the same? If a man were to taunt you with being a part of a mere "ritual mill" how would you justify yourself?

Man's being has been shaped by a Universe that loves repetition and ceremonial; the inspiration to ritualism is everywhere. Night and day everlastingly succeed each other; the four seasons continue their endless circumambulations, like the candidate about the lodge room: the stars move about in their fixed orbits, the tides rise and fall, moons wax and wane, seed-time and harvest come and go, growth is followed by decay, birth is succeeded by death, and even the comet, once deemed the most capricious of all the major objects of creation, has been found to return upon his own path forever. As man gradually became aware of the tirelessness of these cyclic changes, and as he discovered how his own life was linked thereto, he was filled with awe, and himself learned to form processions, to move in the rhythms of the dance, and to devise solemn religious ceremonials in the hope of discovering the secrets of the Universe. Miss Jane Harrison, in her "Ancient Art and Ritual," has given us a lifelike picture of early man in his rude ritualisms and has taught us to see that to ritualize is in man's nature, and that no amount of rationalizing will ever eradicate from his soul his penchant for thus expressing his thoughts and his emotions.

Can you give other examples of repetition in Nature? Did you ever read Herbert Spencer's famous chapter on "rhythm"? What did ritual mean to ancient man? What connection is there between our drama and ancient dancing and ritualism?

Accordingly, the society in which a man finds himself from his birth on is filled with the elements of ceremony. When the child is born we have a christening; when it enters church it is confirmed; it is taught to kneel when it says its prayers; it is instructed how to comport itself at meals; when the wedding day comes, the neighbors are invited for a formal ceremony; and death is sealed by a "service" which must usually be as much like the ceremony in universal use as possible. When we meet or part we shake hands; the gentleman tips his hat to the lady, and we all arise when a guest or a stranger enters the room. Our courts and legislative assemblies have ceremonies of their own, we learn to keep step when we march to war, and the most informal public assembly insists on some semblance of order. All these things are of the essence of ritual, and hard would it be to give a purely rational justification for them, but there is something in us that demands them.

Give other examples of ritualistic elements in society. Can you name the great churches that make a large use of ritual? What part does ritualism play in Roman Catholicism? What other kind of "Catholicisms" are there? Do you enjoy being a part of ceremony? Why?

Although the social psychologist has not yet explained this penchant there is one advantage of it which lies on the surface where we all can see: ritual floats a man out of himself, and gives him a sense of a larger personality. The boy playing in a band, the soldier marching with his company, the youth moving with his athletic team, the adult in a parade - in these, and in numberless similar instances, the individual forgets himself, and is swept by emotions which seem to him grander and more worthy than his own habitual petty private feelings. The enlargement of the individual consciousness into a group consciousness, that, if we care to adopt psychological lingo, is the secret of the prevalence of ritualistic ceremonies. If we will apply this fact to the use of ritual in the Masonic lodge we shall be better able to appreciate and to understand its practice there.

How do you explain the appeal of ritualism? Why, for example, does a Roman Catholic enjoy participating in a ceremony carried on wholly in Latin? Have you had the experience described in the paper as being "floated out of yourself"?

By having a ritual as the basis of lodge work the lodge is saved from the caprices of the individual, and from the dictatorship of some masterful leader. Suppose that on each night that a degree is conferred the degree were to consist of a speech by some brother, or by one of the officers, and that this speech would be new for each occasion. For a time this might be refreshing and novel but after a while the speeches would lose their interest or would become stereotyped, simply because there are so few men that can make a successful speech. The same would hold true of any form of initiation that might dispense with a ritual: the failure of the individual, or the committee, entrusted with the ceremony; or the crankiness of some man determined to have things his own way, or the low quality of it all, would come in time to disgust everybody. The churches in their present day experience illustrate this, for those religious groups that have wholly depended on the preacher to the exclusion of religious ritual are finding their attendance to fall away. The individual soon wears out: but a rich and many-sided ritual, evolved through generations of usage, full of glancing lights, shadows, and mysteries, is never at the mercy of individual caprices or individual failures.

But it must not be supposed that a ritual, at any rate our Masonic ritual, excludes novelty, and the opportunities for the individual to add to the richness of it all, for there is always room for the member of the degree team to improve the work by his better rendition of it, by his vocal interpretation, by masterful gestures, by superiority of costume, and every lodge has opportunities to show its own genius to the full by way of better equipment and furnishings: moreover, for those who are able to give a speech there is usually plenty of opportunity. The repetition of our ritual does no more destroy individuality than did the constant repetition of "Rip Van Winkle" destroy the winsome personality of Joseph Jefferson.

Also it may be noted that a ritual, at any rate such as ours, is far richer in meaning and power than would be the production of any one man; it has been shaped by many hands; its wisdom has come from many minds, and from ages of experience; the art of it has ripened through time like the tints of a mountain-side: there is in it something more profound than any work of one person.

How could Masonic work be carried on without rituals? In what way is ritual an aid to worship? How could your own lodge improve its presentation of the work? How did ritualism arise in Freemasonry ?

It is by means of the ritual that Freemasonry maintains its own identity. Why have some of our Protestant churches changed out of all recognition since their inception? Because it has been left to each leader to shape things very much to suit himself: a succession of private interpretations has overlaid the original message. It would be so with us were it not for our ritual: that ritual of course was changed, but not in the meaning of the message taught, and so gradually, that tonight the young man who takes his First degree will say and do things very much as the young man did several hundred years ago. Also, it is a satisfying thing for the young man tonight to feel that what he is doing in a lodge in the United States some other young man is doing across the world, and other young men, here and elsewhere, will do for ages to come. And when that young man is witnessing in his old age the initiation of his favorite grandson it will bring the tears to his eyes to see and hear just what he saw and heard on the night of his own initiation. Thus it is that it is by means of the ritual that the Fraternity keeps its identity and holds fast to its members the whole world over, and is able to escape dissolution by the washings and the attritions of time.

Furthermore we may say, though there is little room to say more on so rich a subject, that the ever-lasting repetition of the same ritual means that every word becomes associated in the mind of each Mason with varied experiences. The fixed element in the life of the lodge is like a solid rock on which the coral build, or like an old homestead which gathers associations from the generations that have lived in it.

And this ritualistic element, being something that almost any man can learn, excludes no man from participating in the lodge activities. If each lodge meeting meant a speech, or a new program, or some novelty, only a few gifted men could ever take a part. As it is there is not a member so ill-gifted that he cannot at least join the side lines in the battery of acclamation when a candidate is brought to light.

Were there more space for our thoughts twice as much could be said. It is sufficient to recall to our minds how great a treasure we have in our ritual, composed as it is of riches drawn from all parts of the world and from all ages: and to know that it is the Order's great secret of vitality, undying youth, and - this perhaps has not been sufficiently suggested - of a genuine originality of individual development. For there can be no freedom for a man where there is not also the strictest regulations.

If all the stars were to take to novelty, and move freely about like birds in the air; if all the familiar things about us were suddenly to lust after originality and begin rapidly each to become something else, we should have a great insanity and no Universe at all, and in such an imbroglio freedom, spontaneity, originality, individual liberty would vanish, for where order is not freedom cannot be.

Do you agree in saying that Masonry maintains its identity by means of the ritual? How does a great political party maintain its identity? How long does a political party exist as a rule? How long has Masonry lasted? Have you found the Masonic ritual to grow in meaning through seeing it again and again? How would you explain the fact that a fixed order is necessary to individual originality?

Of Symbolism even more can be said than of Ritualism for it has been more universally in use, and is capable of a much wider application. Symbols were the first speech of man. Before words and letters were devised pictures were drawn to convey thoughts, and arbitrary signs were made to stand for many things. Nearly all primitive language is symbolical language, for "the voice of the sign," as Robert Freke Gould has described it, can be understood by children and savages. And in our own present day society, after the use of words has been refined almost infinitely, symbols remain in use on every hand. The crepe on the door is the sign of death; a ring stands for the engagement of a man and a woman, or for their wedding; the lily signifies Easter and immortality, and the employment of buttons, badges, heraldic devices, flags, and what not, is endless. If one could trace a human life through every detail of its existence from birth to death, he would find that human existence is all covered over with symbols.

How do you explain a symbol? Give as many examples as you can of the symbolisms you have encountered during one day's experience. Is a flag a symbol? When did flags first come in use? What did the Greeks and Romans use for flags?

There is nothing arbitrary or simple-minded in the use of a device so universal, neither is there any difficulty in discovering why it is that symbols are so native to us all.

For one thing, a symbol does not exhaust itself so quickly as words. There is mystery and depth in it, an infinity of suggestiveness, an incitement to new approaches of thought. Suppose, for example, that we should substitute a set speech to convey to a candidate the lesson inculcated by the drama of Hiram Abiff! The mere abstract ideas could be thus expressed but how soon they would lose their power over the Man's mind! As it is, no man can witness the symbolical presentation of the tragedy, even for the hundredth time, without finding himself in a new mood, or in the possession of new thoughts. There is something inexhaustible in the symbol, so that it will live long after many languages have died. It keeps saying; to us, "You have rightly guessed this meaning, and that; but I have a thousand other meanings you have not yet hit upon."

This suggests another of the best uses of symbolism. We cannot learn the message of a symbol with a merely passive and receptive mind, because it is of the genius of symbolism to hide as well as to reveal. When a thing is conveyed to us in clear simple words, or in plain pictures, such as one sees in the movies, there is no need that one make a great effort of his own mind to comprehend it all; but when a symbol is put before us, and we have a reason for securing its message to us, our own minds must act, for no symbol wears its meaning on its sleeve. Its value for us is like gold hidden away in the mountain - the miner must dig for it. And that in itself is a virtue, because many men are cursed by the refusal to use their own faculties. They go through the whole of their lives parroting other men's thoughts, and such a life is necessarily lacking in the pleasure of making mental discoveries, which is one of life's sweetest joys.

All the greatest things, love, friendship, death, immortality, religion, patriotism, etc., speak to us through symbols. A flag fluttering at the head of a column of soldiers will stir us as can no oratory: a cross will suggest more about death than any sermon. Perhaps this is because the symbol has so many avenues through which to reach the mind; it partakes of the qualities of the picture, of acts, of sounds, of words, and of ceremony, and because of its wide use and great antiquity there cling about it untold associations.

Have you ever tried to decipher the meanings of our Masonic symbols? How many of those symbols can you name? How would you set about to explain the meaning of the apron? What advantage is there in the fact that each man must think out for himself the meaning of a symbol? Do the ritualistic churches leave it to each member to discover for himself the meaning of their symbols? In what way does Freemasonry differ from those institutions ? What other institutions make a large use of symbolism?

A symbol, unless it is one invented by some individual in a purely arbitrary way, is usually understood everywhere; it speaks a universal language. A circle to us means "infinity," because it has neither beginning nor end. It means the same thing in India and Japan. It meant the same thing to men who lived before the dawn of history. Freemasonry could never have become a worldwide institution had not its ritual been an assemblage of symbols, had not it learned long ago to teach by means of emblems and symbols. If its teachings were set down in a book that book would have to be translated from language to language, never a satisfactory process; speaking in symbols its language is "understood by the people" everywhere.

Also, the symbolical character of the teaching of Freemasonry has tended toward that intellectual tolerance which is one of its glories. There can be no dogmatic and official interpretation of a symbol to compel the unwilling assent of any mind; the symbol's message is, by virtue of its very nature, fluid and free, so that every man has a right to think it out for himself. Of Masonic teachers and scholars there have been many - Oliver, Preston, Pike, Mackey, and others equally as honorable to our history - and these have given us noble interpretations of Masonry, but no Mason is ever compelled to accept them unless he choose. In a great Order which teaches by means of the living "voice of the sign" there never can be a pope.

Which reminds us that symbolism in itself is no infallible thing, and not the whole of wisdom. Just as there are good books and bad, and good men and bad, so are there good and bad symbols, and each one must keep toward all symbolisms an active and critical mind. We must always discriminate.

Did you ever read Rudyard Kipling's story, "The Man Who Would be King"? If so, how does it teach the fact that symbols are a universal language? How would you yourself illustrate that fact? in what way does symbolism make for intellectual toleration? Are any of the Masonic symbols failures as such? Are there any you would care to have dispensed with? Why?

After studying the philosophy of symbolism under the leadership of the foregoing hints it will be well for the student or the study club to investigate a further question: What rule shall, we go by in trying to interpret Masonic symbols? What was said of each member's right to think out the symbols for himself did not imply, of course, that he ever has a right to interpret a Masonic symbol without thinking, or that he can ever discover a true interpretation without due regard for what others have thought of it. That procedure would be not free thought but an absence of thought. I myself believe, and have found in practice the soundness of, the historical principle of interpretation. By this is meant that if we undertake to interpret some symbol we must first try to learn what that symbol has always meant to the Fraternity during times past. If we ask ourselves, for example, what is the meaning of the square and compass, we should try to discover when that symbol came into use in the Fraternity; why it thus came into use; what it then meant, and then we should try to learn what the Fraternity has understood by this symbol during the subsequent centuries. This would save us from an interpretation based on ignorance, or arbitrariness, or our own crotchets, and it would also throw new light for us on what Freemasonry as a whole means.

How have you interpreted the Masonic symbols? Have you any rule to go by? Does the use of a rule of interpretation interfere with the right of private interpretation? If your son were to be initiated into the First degree tomorrow how would you go about explaining to him what it all means? How would it benefit the whole Order if all its members were to undertake to find out what the symbols mean?

PART VI
INITIATION AND SECRECY

MANY a man has left the Masonic lodge room after the last night of his initiation with the feeling that what he has seen and heard has all been very interesting and impressive but also very queer: it has been so entirely different from the other experiences of his life that it all seems unreal, a strange piece of formality, as if somebody had devised it as an ornate but formal way of getting a man inducted into Masonry. It is no wonder that many who go away with such impressions never again take much interest in the ceremonies of initiation. What such a man needs is to have brought home to him that which is the main contention of this present series of studies, namely, that initiation, along with all the more important features of our Craft, is not a strange thing arbitrarily devised by somebody for ornamental and ceremonial purposes, but normal, and natural, and inevitable, just as natural as the blowing wind or the falling snow. Initiation is something that has been in universal use from the beginning of the world and it is therefore as human a piece of business as anything that we do, albeit not so common perhaps.

How many reasons can you think of for the general indifference to the ritual among members? Did you accept the ritualistic part of your initiation as a perfunctory ceremony? Does the ritual sound to you like a manufactured thing? Do you believe, as Albert Pike seemed sometimes to believe, that certain things in the ritual were devised to conceal Masonic teachings ?

Instead of approaching the matter in the abstract it is well to begin by observing just what happens to a candidate during the process of his initiation into Freemasonry. First of all, he signs a paper setting for certain important facts about himself: then he participates in the "work" for three nights: he binds himself by a solemn obligation to do certain things and not do certain other things: he takes the oath of secrecy which covers the ceremonies and also what may be said or done in lodge at any time: he contracts to give financial support to the Craft according to its laws thereon: he enters into a new relation with a large group of men who have been similarly initiated and sworn; and he places himself for life under a set of very definite and very noble influences. One could add to this list but as it is it is sufficient to recall to our minds just what is actually done through the process of initiation; and it is perfectly plain that, except for some words and actions in the ceremonies, there is nothing in all this to give anybody the slightest feeling that it is strange or abnormal: it is all as real and as natural as living. This is something worth remembering because many who have approached the subject of initiation from a merely abstract and theoretical position are very apt to give us impossible theories of the matter, land us in difficulties, and make us believe that Masonic initiation is something unnatural to human beings: as a matter of actual fact it is nothing of the kind.

I have said that during the ceremonies incidental to initiation some things are done and said that do see queer to any man when first he encounters them. But even these elements in our "mysteries" are not there for any fantastic or unreal purpose: they are there because we have inherited them from the past, and because they still have for us such valuable meanings that we continue to hold to them. If there is anything in the ritual that seems fantastic to a man he needs only to study the history of the same to have such an impression obliterated.

The unfortunate thing is that many candidates pass through the entire process of initiation without being affected to any depth at all. Why is this? Very often it is the candidate's own fault. Before entering, or even seeking to enter, such an institution as Freemasonry he should learn something about it; at least a little of its history, and as much as possible about its present activities. And then, after he has passed through the initiation ceremonies, he should stop long enough to find out what it all means. A man to be impressed by anything must do his own part: nothing can act as a substitute for his own brains, feelings, and actions. Moreover, Masonic initiation is a blessing, carrying with it many precious privileges, and it is therefore worth something of an effort on the part of a man who seeks it.

How would you define "initiation"? Can you furnish examples of initiation drawn from general society outside secret orders? What do you consider the most important features of Masonic initiation? Do you consider the obligation legally binding on a member? Did initiation strike you as being "queer"? If so, what parts of it? What did you know about Freemasonry before you sought admission to it? Do you recall anything in the ritual which assumes that you made a study of Masonry before submitting your application ?

In all other cases the poor effect of initiation is due to the carelessness of the lodge. A ritual cannot be satisfactorily administered in a mechanical way, as if all one had to do was to turn the crank of a mill. Nor can it ever be a cut-and-dried thing which needs no thought and initiative behind it. No lodge has a right to shove a man through three degrees and then turn him loose without first endeavoring to instruct him in the meaning of it all, without trying to bring home to him what it was designed to do. The whole process should be made one of the most crucial experiences of the candidate's life, one that he can never forget, one that will change him to the centre of his being, else it is not a real initiation at all, but an imitation.

For consider what takes place inside a man when initiation has been a success. The word itself suggests a "new birth." The experience, whenever it actually occurs, is a profound one. It is like the crisis of adolescence when a boy finds himself passing through a mysterious change that throws his whole being into turmoil; he grows moody; his beard makes its appearance; his voice changes; he gets a new expression in his face; his muscles develop; his interests change; he begins to take more interest in the opposite sex; he is no longer a boy but a young man. Or it is like the moral and spiritual change which comes over a man who passes through the religious experience known as "conversion" or "regeneration"; he finds himself with a new set of interests; he behaves differently to his family and his fellows; he forms new habits, such as prayer and church attendance; he has a new feeling about God; new beliefs about the great questions that concern man; he calls himself a "new" man. He has been initiated into the religious life, which is to him a new world of experience, and he can never again become what he was, even though all these new interests fade away.

Can you furnish examples of a "new birth" other than adolescence and religious "conversion"? What brought about such conversion? Can a genuine change in a man's life be brought about by a mere ceremony, a mere formality? If many Masons in your lodge are worthless as Masons how do you explain their lack of the Masonic life? Why did initiation fail in their cases?

Masonic initiation is intended to be quite profound and revolutionizing an experience. As a result of it the candidate should become a new man: he should have a new range of thought; a new feeling about mankind; a new idea about God; a new confidence in immortality; a new passion for brotherhood, a new generosity and charity. The whole purpose of the ritual, of the symbols, of all that is done and said, is solemnly to bring about such a transformation in the man. If initiation does not accomplish something of this it is a failure; if it does accomplish it, that fact should forever silence those who have looked upon it as an elaborate and expensive piece of formalism.

Have you ever heard men argue against the rightness of secrecy in Masonry? what arguments have you heard? how did you answer them? What part does secrecy play in your business? in your home? in your friendships? Why did Operative Masons hedge themselves about with secrecy? What is a "trade" secret? Did you ever try to remove the hoodwink of Masonic ignorance from a brother Mason? how did you go about it?

Secrecy is so prominent a characteristic of Freemasonry that often in literature we find the latter word used as a synonym of the former, as when we read how a circle of friends were so intimate that there was a "kind of freemasonry" among them. To some this is most objectionable because they deem it beneath the dignity of a great Order to conceal its functionings behind so opaque a veil: or they think that what must be so effectually hidden must contain some taint, or have anti-social influences. "If it is good and noble," so they say, "why hide your light under a bushel? if your hidden actions are reprehensible then is all your secrecy an elaborate hypocrisy! or it may be that all your secrecy is merely an elaborate bit of child's play designed to appeal to curiosity mangers. In any event our best public institutions, the church, school, public hospitals, libraries, and even our political governments, have no need of such a veil." The fallacy underlying these objections is that the objectors do not know that Masonic secrecy is a peculiar kind of secrecy designed and preserved expressly for the needs of such an institution.

Anyhow, there is nothing objectionable or unfamiliar about secrecy; it is a human necessity found everywhere, and often where it is not apparently in evidence it will be found on examination to equal or even exceed that which lies about the gateways of our Fraternity. Nothing is more zealously guarded than the home. The directors of a business corporation keep their deliberations to themselves. Friendship is based on mutual confidence and that means much secrecy. Governments are very public in function but they are still obliged to carry on many of their activities behind the scenes. Indeed, what would life be without this honorable kind of concealment! how would any man endure to go about in the world with all his inner life exposed to view like the goods in a show window!

Freemasonry partakes of the nature of this more common kind of secrecy, but there is secrecy and secrecy, and one variety of it is one about which we do not often think: I refer to that which is as yet unknown to us, not because we are shut out from it, but because we are not yet prepared or equipped to learn it. Music is a terra incognito to one who knows not one note from another, and can not recognize a tune. Literature is a vast unknown to the illiterate. Chemistry, physics, geology, astronomy, or any of the sciences, is a complete mystery to those who have no knowledge of them. The nature of Freemasonry is also a mystery for it is revealed only to those initiated into it. They are not hidden from us by any arbitrary authority: they are hidden because we wear the hoodwink of ignorance. Much of our Masonic secrecy is of this character. As a matter of fact it is surprising how little of it there is that can not be published to outsiders: the contents of this journal from month to month bear witness to that! but there is a vast deal of it that remains unknown even to its own initiates because they have as yet made no effort to learn it.

Also, Masonic secrecy exists for certain definite purposes. The Fraternity itself exists in order to keep fixed on a man a certain set of influences, and in order to bring about certain changes in the world, etc.: its secrecy is a means to that end, and helps to make such a purpose possible. If a lodge room were as open to the general public as a street corner all that goes specifically by the name of Masonry would necessarily vanish and the very purpose for which the Order exists would be defeated.

Experience teaches this fact as well as reflection. The Order has existed in one form or another for we know not how many centuries, and it has always been a secret society. Other modern fraternities have found secrecy equally necessary. So also with fraternities in earlier times. The Mysteries hedged themselves about in the most elaborate fashion. The Collegia held their meetings behind tyled doors. The Christian church, in at least one period of its history, did the same; and so did the numberless guilds of Medieval Europe.

Has Freemasonry anything to conceal from its enemies? what? What things in Masonry, according to your own understanding of it, are necessarily kept secret? Could Masonry continue to exist without secrecy? Why? What are the attractions of secrecy to the human mind? Can you name a great political party that once existed in the United States that was organized as a secret society? why was it thus organized? why did it abandon its secrecy? Would you call the Order of the Jesuits a secret society?

There is a psychology of secrecy, the discussion of which is recommended to students and to study clubs though little space is available for it here. What we value we instinctively guard. Curtains are drawn before the more intimate things of life. Even religion, to a majority of individuals, is a thing for the private rather than for the public stage, and many a man would rather be thought an infidel than be caught at prayer. In all these, and in scores of cases like them, secrecy is used as a screen whereby to protect sensitive feelings. In many other equally familiar cases secrecy employed to awaken the desire to explore, the curiosity to know; it stimulates a man to make search for that which is presented to him as a mystery. One may see Masonic secrecy affecting the minds of brethren in the lodge room in both these ways: some are happy to be there because they can give expression to thoughts, to ideals, and to aspirations, often religious, among trusted brethren: and some are there because the veil thrown about our mysteries has enticed them to try to lift it.

To my own mind the noblest effect of Masonic secrecy is found in the atmosphere of kindliness which it throws about all the operations of brotherly aid and charity. The unfortunate member is often helped almost without himself knowing whence his succor comes; there is no publishing abroad of the affliction; the thing is not bragged about; usually the object of this charity does not even make an application: like the stretching forth of a gentle hand he feels himself supported in such wise that his pride needs not to sink to the level of his fortunes. If Masonic secrecy did nothing else it would be abundantly justified to every delicate and charitable mind.

While keeping all this in mind it is also well to remember that, after all, Masons themselves sometimes do not understand this, the secrecy of the Craft, aside from the single matter of its charity, is almost wholly concerned with method rather than with matter. If one will carefully consider the oath of secrecy he made while taking his obligation he will find that he is not in anyway to reveal to others aught of the initiatory ceremony, or of what may be said in lodge: but he is not sworn to keep secret that which Freemasonry really is! Its principles, its history, its spirit, its ideals, its purposes and programs, he may publish to the world and the more he publishes them the better.

Just what does the obligation to secrecy cover? Do you know about the charitable activities of your own lodge? Do you believe the charity should be secret? why? Could public charity be similarly veiled? how? Can you think of a single teaching or principle of Masonry that has not been given to the world over and over again? Can you explain why the whole Order would pass out of existence if its secrecy were to be destroyed?

PART VII
MASONIC ETHICS

A MAN can never hurt or help natural forces. He can spread his sail, but that does not affect the wind. He can overturn the sod with his plow but the sod does not scream back at him with pain. He can send his wireless messages through space but that does not change the structure of the atmosphere. A man does not have much choice in his dealings with nature. If he steps from a roof he immediately falls to the earth, whatever be his opinions of gravity. The sun shines, night darkens, seasons change, rain falls, the ocean moves through its tides, but the will of man has nothing to do with all this.

A man's relationship with his fellow men is very different. He can hurt or help them, bless or curse. What he says may change the course of another's fortunes: what he does may be a matter of life and death to a fellow. And all that he does to and with his fellows is largely under the control of his own will, for he can choose to act or not to act, to think or not to think, to speak or not to speak, and he can so choose when he knows that his thoughts, words, or deeds will influence them greatly one way or another. This is also true of a man's own self, and his relationship with himself: he can make his own person the object of his thoughts and acts for good or ill, and, as these thoughts and acts are of his own choosing, he is responsible, and they become a part of his conduct. All the ways in which a man affects himself, and in which men affect each other, for which men are responsible, comprise the materials of morality, of which ethics is the science.

Freemasonry has its own interpretation of the principles of morality. It has its own ideals of human conduct. For reasons of its own it emphasizes certain duties, and encourages certain ideals. In order to persuade men to act in a certain way it brings to bear up them certain influences and strives to neutralize other influences which may oppose its purposes. It knows what it wants a man to be, and human society in general to be, and it bends its efforts towards that end. Masonic Ethics is ethics studied from this particular point of view, in the light of Masonic principles and ideals, and in behalf of Masonic purposes. It is the study of ethics as it bears on Masonry and of Masonry as it bears on ethics. Such a study bulks large in literature of the Craft, in its philosophy, in its teachings, its ritual, and its traditions, because Masonry is above all other things a moralistic institution, which strives to realize on earth a definite ideal of conduct, both private and public. It is unfortunate that no modern Masonic scholar has yet attempted to make a careful study of Masonic history and literature in order to build a System of Masonic Ethics, in the same way that numberless other students have built up systems of Christian ethics, or Chinese ethics, or Jewish, etc.

Is there a difference between "morality" and "ethics"? Do you believe that every man is responsible for his acts? Could a man's acts be blameworthy or praiseworthy if be had no choice about them? What has the human will to do with morality? Does the Bible define morality? Does it anywhere define righteousness? How would you define "right" and "wrong"?

The majority of men know as little of moral science as of any other science, and their conceptions of "right" and "wrong" are, accordingly, often as valueless as their conceptions of astronomy, or physics. From tradition, from the church, or from hearsay, without ever having submitted it to careful scrutiny of sound thinking, they have accepted into their minds a rough code of morals. This code consists, for the most part, of two contrasted lists of actions: one, of actions permitted; the other, of actions forbidden. Whenever the question arises, Is such and such a proposed action good or bad? they refer the matter to their "lists" and act accordingly. A man says to himself, Shall I gamble? Shall I send money to the missionaries? Shall I tell this untruth to my neighbor? Shall I use drugs? If he finds gambling to be listed with his mental category of things forbidden he will look upon it as a sin. If missionary gifts are in the list of things permitted, such gifts are right, etc.

This procedure works satisfactorily until the man comes into conflict with an entirely different code. One example of this will suffice. A Frenchman, let it be supposed a Christian also, finds that drinking wine is permitted by his own moral code. An American Baptist, on the other hand, finds wine among the things most violently forbidden by his own code. Who, or what, is to decide between them? The Frenchman may appeal to the authority of the New Testament: so may the Baptist. The Frenchman may say, My church has long ago decided this matter: the Baptist may reply, Mine also has decided the matter. If the Frenchman appeals to the tradition of his group, the Baptist can retort in the same way, and to an opposite conclusion. It is plain that this simple-minded "list" or code system of morality is one that breaks down the moment a man seeks the ground that lies beneath it.

This is nothing other than the age-old search for the seat of authority in morals. When a man is in moral predicament, and does not know whether or not a given course of action is right or wrong, to what final authority can he refer his problem? In the writer's opinion there can be but one answer. The human experience of the individual is the one final authority in morals. If a man does something that injures his own body; or needlessly, destroys something of human value; or hurts another in any way; or deliberately makes himself or others unhappy, that man does wrong. Wrong is whatever hurts human life, or destroys human happiness; right is whatever helps human life, and tends to sustain or increase human happiness. There is but one way to learn what it is that hurts or helps and that is by experience, and whenever one is not sure what experience has to say he is obliged to make a moral experiment. Acts are not right or wrong intrinsically, but according as their effects are hurtful or helpful. The purpose of right living is not in order to render obedience to some code, or to some supposed authority, but to enable a man to live richly, healthful and happy. A wise man may therefore often do something that may not be approved by others, but the man who does something which his own experience shows to be hurtful is a fool.

Does the Masonic Ritual anywhere define "righteousness"? How would you describe "Masonic ethics"? What duties are emphasized by the Craft? What ideals are encouraged? Is there such a thing as a

Masonic Code? What is it? How do you yourself determine whether or not a thing is "right"? What is the conscious? Do you consider it a separate faculty? Have you been unconsciously making use the of mental "lists" of right and wrong actions? Is that the wisest moral procedure? Or should a man prefer to trust his own "moral judgment" from time to time? What is meant by "moral judgment"? Are you acquainted with any Masonic book that interprets Masonic Ethics?.

This does not mean that a man can safely trust to his own experience alone: far otherwise, for often a man's own experience is too meager to be of any value. Others have lived longer or more richly than he, or more wisely, and he can heed their counsels. Others, by virtue of some special training, may better understand the effects of a given course of action, and consequently have a right to direct conduct, as a physician has a right to prescribe remedies.

Certain courses of action have always and everywhere been found to be hurtful or harmful. Willfully to deceive another will be found hurtful in China as in America, in the first century as well as in the twentieth: so also with habits of gluttony or intemperance that destroy health; with extravagance, laziness, cruelty, etc. One can't conceive of any social condition under which men would not find these things to make for unhappiness. These permanent verdicts of human experience become at last crystallized into principles which nobody questions, and these principles, taken together, comprise a system of morality. But, even so, all such principles are found to root in human experience and its verdicts. Should the constitution of man come under some mysterious change so that men would be made happier by gluttony, and life made richer and stronger, then would gluttony become a good and not a bad.

The vast majority of moral problems, however, have not been, and never can be, permanently settled: always the individual, so far as these things are concerned, must decide for himself. Is the use of alcohol injurious? Some physicians say it is, others say not: some men seem to drink with impunity as well as pleasure: others get headaches and nights of sleeplessness after a few drinks: in such a case the individual must decide for himself, and, so long as the question remains strictly a matter of private experience, he has no right to decide for another. The exception, of course, is when others are involved, such as in drunk driving. It is not the submission to a traditional code of action that sets one apart as a man of principle and character; the strong man, from the moral point of view, is he who, when experience decides, abides the verdict, though it may oppose many selfish interests and interfere with many cherished pleasures.

How have you been in the habit of adjusting your own moral code to the moral code of others when the two conflict? How would you settle the controversy between the Frenchman and the Baptist given in the text? Do you believe the Bible to be the final court of appeal in moral questions? If so, why? How would you justify that position to an intelligent Buddhist, Mohammedan, Confucianist, or to one who rejects the supernatural character of the Bible? Are all the moral teachings of the Bible consistent with themselves?

The test of experience is equally valid when applied to the more religious and idealistic questions of human conduct: self-sacrifices, heroisms, martyrdoms, these, like the more commonplace matters of daily life, are approved or condemned according as they make for or against human life. The monks who went off to live cenobite lives in the Thebaid considered themselves very holy men, but the verdict of the subsequent centuries has been against them, for such a life proved itself to be harmful to the healthfulness and happiness of the world. The thousands who went away to the Crusades considered themselves divinely commissioned, but today a saner judgment, though it admires the element of heroism in the Crusaders, condemns the enterprise as a whole as having been a useless piece of costly fanaticism. Emerson and Thoreau, inflamed by the enthusiasms of the hour, hailed John Brown as the hero of the nation after his wild attempt on Harper's Ferry: James Ford Rhodes, in the light of the full consequences of the old Puritan's campaign, shows that John Brown let loose a train of bloody and unfortunate consequences, from which the slaves themselves were the chief sufferers. All this is to say that ideals, aspirations, heroisms, self-sacrifices, and all other similar acts and aims are not in themselves any more "righteous" than are other more familiar matters of conduct, and that they are to be adjudged "right" or "wrong" only in light of the conditions under which they are done and the consequences that flow from them.

This philosophizing about moral conduct is of great value to us in our periods of leisure and reflection but a man can't stop to philosophize, often he cannot even stop to weigh probabilities, and to balance motives, while he is in the midst of his daily living, for usually decisions must be made on the spot, and often they are made unconsciously, like an instinctive action. The thing that determines a man in all such decisions is his moral "nature," and that nature is the man's fixed system of habits, reactions, judgments, emotions, etc., that has been built out of all his past experience. A good man is one who has in the past so lived that he habitually acts so as to be happy himself and make others happy (the word "happy" here is used in its widest possible meaning). He may now and then do something that he knows to be wrong, but his "nature," the constant bias of his will, is toward those things that make for the welfare of human life. A bad man is one whose very nature is such that he instinctively does things that hurt others or himself, though he often be capable of tenderness, self-sacrifices, or so momentary nobility.

A man acts from his nature. This fact is recognized in the account of the conversation Jesus had with Nicodemus whom the Master told that he had first be "born again." This phrase has passed into theology as the doctrine of "regeneration," or "new birth," it is a sound doctrine, for many men are so ingrained with badness that their whole nature must be radically changed before they can be trusted to live in harmony and happiness with their fellows.

This doctrine of a "new birth" seems to lie at heart of Masonry's great drama of Hiram Abiff. Masonic interpreters have differed greatly among themselves as to the meaning of that acted parable, but they nearly all hold in common the belief that it somehow means that, in order to be a just and true brother a man must be "born again" so that his nature is changed to act in unison with a new world. How can this be brought about? It is one of the points where morality melts into religion, for nearly all the religions have applied themselves to creating a new nature in man, they all seek to do it by bringing Divine Power to be upon the individual. Freemasonry is here at one with religion, for it also resorts to prayer, to the seeking the will of God. It also makes use of the powers brotherhood, of reasoning, of ritual, and all the offices of fraternity. The whole ceremony is in itself an attempt to create a new nature in the candidate, and it is also, from another point of view, a symbol of those influences in this world which have such regenerative powers; these influences, of course, are numberless, and many of them have no direct connection with religion, as for example, the affection for a parent, education, misfortune, etc., any one of which may, under certain circumstances, bring about a profound change in some individual's moral nature.

What has been said of the individual's moral life may be said, in some degree or other, of society at large. How is a great social institution judged? By social experience: by its influence on the life of the community. If some institution, however long established, or however venerated, begins to cause unhappiness among men, dissension, unrest, poverty, or what not, that institution, though it may be sanctioned by the law of the land, becomes evil, and all right thinking men must become its enemies. Whatever social force makes against the welfare of men and women, that social force is evil, though it wear the name of morality itself; whatever social force makes for the welfare of society, that is good, though it be as new as the morning. That an institution is old, or religious, or legal, a fact to be taken into careful consideration, but such a fact has no weight as against the plain influences of that institution as it works among men. For this reason there is such a thing as a social morality. It is the study of social forces in the light of their results and effects in the community; it is the moral appraisal of social institutions. It is the fostering of the forces that make for common welfare, and the opposition of those that make against life.

Always, morality is for the sake of men and women: it is here in order that they may have life and have it more abundantly. Each man lives in a community where he acts and is acted upon, where he is influenced by others and himself influences others. His own nature is a bundle of energies and influences upon which happiness depends. To so adjust one's self to others, to so learn to govern one's self, and to so adjust one's life to the forces of nature, in order that one's life may be full, rich, happy, that is the aim of morality. It is also the aim of Masonry, for that great institution exists in order that men may live happily together and in order that human life, individual or social, may evermore rise to high and higher issues.

What is meant by "experience"? How many thing, can you think of that have always and everywhere been wrong? Has slavery, according to the "experience doctrine" given in this work, always been wrong? Has polygamy? Make a careful study of some important moral problem, such as the problem of the double sex standard, in the light of this doctrine. Do you believe that John Brown did more harm than good? How would you decide on the prohibition question in the light of the interpretation of right and wrong given in the paper? Have you ever been "born again"? Are men ever born again as the result of Masonic influences? What is Masonry's ideal for human life? For society at large? Would it make men and women happier?

PART VIII
EQUALITY

IT IS not often that one of the subjects of speculative thought becomes the burning issue of the hour but that is what happened in our own national history between 1850 and 1861 with the doctrine of equality. The whole matter, needless to say, was brought to the front by the slavery issue. Anti-slavery orators never wearied of reminding their southern friends that the fathers of the nation, in their Declaration of Independence, had openly proclaimed "that all men are created equal": if that is true, they argued, then Negroes deserve the rights of citizenship, for Negroes are men. The pro-slavery advocates retorted by saying; that the fathers of the country, many of them, had themselves been slave holders, and that they had really meant to say that "all men are created equal except Negroes." He who reads through the more important debates on that subject - such a one will be richly rewarded - will learn how exceedingly difficult it is to frame any definition of human equality that will at once do justice to things as they are and to things as they ought to be. Equality is an aspiration, (in Masonry as elsewhere) a hope, a dream, an, ideal, hard to capture in a net of words, difficult to envisage by the mind, and one must remain content after all his thinking about the matter he has not yet been able to think it through.

It is as difficult to arrive at a clear conception of equality from the history of Masonry as it is from the history of this nation. The old Craft Mason did not have any equality except in a very special sense. His guild was a helpless part of an aristocratic social order. He himself had a place in his own guild determined by the most rigorous regulations laid down from above. The guilds themselves were graded in importance, and the members inside each guild were held fast in a similar hierarchy. There is no evidence to show that at any time prior to 1717 any form of Masonry explicitly taught and enforced the doctrine. Subsequent to 1717 the doctrine has come to the fore, and in some countries has almost occupied the first place among Masonic teachings. But ever, so there have been many exceptions. In the Masonry of Latin countries equality has not, for obvious reasons, been very much emphasized. Even in England it has never had a very rigorous application to the social classes of an aristocratic society. When the Earl of Carnovan inducted King Edward VII into his seat as Grand Master he was careful to remind that Potentate that English Masonry had never been subversive of the monarchical system as it had been in other countries.

It is in France and in America that we find the Masonic doctrine of equality most in evidence, and most influential. The part played by Masonry in the French Revolution is, and perhaps will ever remain, pretty much of a mystery. But there is sound evidence to prove that Masonry had much to do with convincing the French masses that they had rights of their own. To this day liberty and democracy is widely understood in France in the equalitarian sense. "Liberty, Fraternity, Equality" is a slogan that has not yet lost its power of appeal.

But it is in our own land that equality has played its major part in Masonic history. It may be that it as Masonry itself (though this point is hotly disputed) that wrote into the Declaration the words "All men be created equal." It is certain that Masonry had with the strain of equalitarianism that runs the Constitution. And it is certain that at present moment equality and Masonry are almost synonymous in many, many minds.

How many kinds of guilds were there? Was Operative Masonry a guild? Do you consider England a democratic country where equality is a fact? What do you know about the connection between Masonry and the French Revolution?

I have my own theory as to what Equality means a Masons, and I shall give it: but I give it as nothing other than my own private opinion, and not as an expression of a generally held formulation of the doctrine. I wish that such a general interpretation could be made because Masonic thinking demands it. Until we can work out such an interpretation the whole matter will ever remain as foggy as it seems to be now (if one may from Masonic literature, speeches, and journalism), and not many Masons will understand what is it is said that all Masons "meet upon the level."

It is easiest to approach the subject by a process of elimination. By equality we cannot mean that all men are equal in the original endowment of their nature. There are big men and little men, and we all know that in many cases a big man "was born that way," and that a little man cannot become big by ever so much effort. Why this is so is a mystery, and appears to be (though it doubtless is not) a fundamental injustice in the very structure of the universe. I had brought to mind recently while reading the third volume of "The History of the United States" by James Ford Rhodes, wherein he carries through several pages a comparison of Lincoln and McClellan. McClellan was spiteful, vainglorious, and ill-mannered; he was a good organizer but he did not have the courage which naturally belongs to a general. He treated the President with rudeness, and wrote to his wife in such strains of pride as made her believe the fate of the Union depended on him alone. Lincoln was a great incarnation of human power who could be magnanimous, meek, patient for that very reason. In contrasting the two men one cannot help but believe that the sundering difference was a matter of original nature, and that at birth Lincoln was more of a human being than McClellan. An inequality like that, one that goes down to the roots of being, is one that is hard to reconcile with our sense of the evenhanded justice of Nature. But the fact is there, and it is everywhere, for no two men have the same aboriginal endowments, let abstract theorists say what they may.

We cannot say that men are equal in nature: neither can we say that they are equal, or can be equal, in opportunity. That may possibly happen in small circles all the members of which live under the same conditions, as in the case of a family, or a neighborhood, but it is untrue of mankind when viewed in the large. The Australian Bushmen, to take an extreme example, never can have the opportunities for education, for wealth, for pleasure, fame, what not, as are enjoyed by the average American youth. Men should have equal opportunities but they do not have them. They never can have them because the earth itself varies too much over its surface ever to make it possible for all men everywhere to be born into equal opportunities for the goods of life.

Men are not born equal in abilities. On this it is not needful to say much because that kind of inequality is one that confronts us everywhere. It used to be the fashion among theorists to teach that if only all men could receive the same education and have the same chances at wealth, and live under equal laws, and be freed from unnatural restrictions, all would come up to the same average. Horace Mann firmly believed that if all the boys and girls of this nation could get into college all of them would turn out scholars, proficient in Greek, Latin, and the arts. But those who have had any experience with boys and girls in college know that nothing is more certain and unvarying than differences of ability. One student, no matter how hard he tries, cannot master mathematics; another seems to be mathematical by nature.

In the last place - there is no need further to multiply instances - there can be no such thing as social equality, if by that term one means social uniformity. Social classes there are, and always will be, because social needs and instincts are so various. If a social class (I use the word in its largest sense) is based on caste, or aristocratic privilege, or any other kind of special privilege, then it is an evil. But there are many social classes that are based not on the principle of the superiority of one group of persons to another but upon the fact of difference among men. I shall use a very homely example. In a small town a group of fifty persons organize themselves into a literary club, and in the activities of such a club meet each other socially, get acquainted with each other, and all share in the common enjoyment of literary art. Let us suppose, for clearness of illustration, that admittance to this club rests purely on the desire to share in the study of literature. It is plain that there will be a great number of persons in the community who will never desire membership, because in every community there are so many who care nothing for literature. This example, as I said above, is of trivial character in itself, but, it may serve to remind us of how many social gradations, classes, cliques, clubs, etc., there are everywhere which rest not on any fact of superiority but upon the fact of the difference of interests, tastes, and aims among people. As long as such differences exist (which will probably be as long as there is a human race) there will never come a time when such social groupings will vanish away, and there will consequently never come a time when all men will enjoy the same social advantages. To work for the advent of such a social state, as the Communists have ever done, as in the case of Owen, Fourier, St. Simon, etc., is to strive for the impossible. Such social communism is not equality in any possible sense.

What, then, is Equality? Instead of attempting any exhaustive definition, I shall make a generalization concerning it, and then trust to a series of examples to do the defining for me. The statement is follows:

Every man is entitled to the right, equal to the right enjoyed by other men, to the unhindered and normal functionings of his own nature.

Sir Isaac Newton had a great intellect, one of the very greatest, all historians agree, that has ever appeared on the earth. My intellect cannot in any sense be spoken of as equal to his. Nevertheless I claim the same right to use my intellect, such as it is, that he enjoyed; and he, if he were living, would have no right whatsoever, merely because of his own superiority, to deny me the prerogatives of thought. For him to do so, and for me to submit to such abasement would be a crime against nature. The right to use the mind is for all men everywhere and always the same right, whatever may be the inequalities of mental ability. Whenever this right is interfered with, or controlled in the interests of some clique or class, as has often happened, society suffers, individuals suffer, and a wrong is done that merits condign punishment.

The same thing holds good of practical ability. William Morris had an extraordinarily versatile genius. He could weave tapestry, carve wood, paint pictures, write poetry, make speeches, model in clay, print books, and a score of things beside, and do all with rare skill. There are few of us who could claim any such ability, but even so, we have the same right to use our powers that Morris had to use his. In that fundamental and all-important regard, William Morris was no better than the most awkward apprentice in his workshops.

Every one of us is social by nature, and nearly every one of us appreciates the rare privilege of friendship. But some men seem to have a genius for friendship. Theodore Watts-Dunton, comparatively unknown himself, was the centre of a circle of friends almost every one of whom became famous in some line. Our own Charles Eliot Norton, than whom no rarer spirit has ever dwelt in this land, numbered among his close friends such men as Ruskin, Carlyle, Emerson, Lowell, George William Curtis, Charles Darwin, Leslie Stephen, and nobody knows how many more such outstanding personalities. You and I may number our friends on the fingers of one hand, and they may be the humblest imaginable so far as attainments go, but for all that each of us has the right to friends, the same right as that enjoyed by Watts-Dunton and Eliot Norton. Such a statement may seem banal enough, but there are places in the world now, and have been many places in the past, where social life has been so rigidly classified and graded that custom and aristocratic dictation have made impossible to all but a few the unhindered exercise of so fundamental a thing in human nature as the cultivation of friendship.

The right of human equality has been often violated, it seems, in religion, the one field in which men should enjoy the largest measure of it. What a tale of unrightful usurpation, tyranny, and aristocracy has been the history of the world's churches. One no sooner thinks of the matter than examples flock to the mind in unmanageable numbers. During one great period of their history the Egyptian people were entirely abased beneath the feet of a priestly hierarchy that crushed out in the masses the very instincts of worship, or made use of that instinct for the advantage of their own class. After Buddha had unveiled to the eyes of his people the sacredness of each individual soul before the ineffable and eternal realities of the universe, the Brahmans came back with their castes and their engines of oppression and the people lost once again all uses of their own religious faculties. Jesus came forth to make each man know himself as a son of God, bound together in the great circle of brethren, but after time went on, and the priestly leaven had its opportunities to work, it required a Lutheran revolution to restore to Christians the "liberty of a Christian man." The old lady across the street, who reads her Bible morning and evening, who arises and retires with prayer, and, who lives in her humble and unlearned way such a religious life as she is capable of conceiving of, is worlds removed in religious faculty from a Buddha, a Jesus, a Luther: but she is as much entitled as they to think her poor religious thoughts, and to lead her life of little pieties.

From this it will be seen that equality is not a utopian theory which men have dreamed as being desirable in this harsh world. Far from it! Equality is a necessity of our nature, without which we live mutilated, unhappy lives. It is a necessity, when properly understood, like food, clothing, and shelter. He who robs men of that equality which Nature ordains is committing a crime against human beings. He does something that must necessarily be followed by tragic consequences, as is true of the violation of any other condition made necessary by Nature herself. It is because this that the doctrine is not a mere plaything for erudites but a pressing problem for every man, however busy he may be.

"But," some reader may here rightfully interject, is all, very good, and nobody will deny that equality is a right but what about equality as a fact? One needs only look about him to see that even the simple and basic equality which you have described, is not being enjoyed by the masses of people to any degree at all!"

"True enough," I should reply, "but you have merely stated the complementary fact (complementary, is, to what I have hitherto said) that equality is a task as well as a right, and it is precisely because equality is a right that it is for us all a task" "By that I mean, that if we are clear in our mind that every man is justly entitled to a reasonable measure of equality then it is for us all, insofar as we are good Masons and citizens, to see that every man gets it. To see that man gets it is precisely one of the great missions in which Masonry is engaged.

Give other examples in which men have been denied religious equality. How would you define religious equality? What does Masonry teach about religious equality?

Let us consider a moment equality before the law. There was a time in England when only the rich had access to the protection of the "law" at all, and when priesthood had its own courts where priest administered the law to priest. Poor men were arrested without warrant; sentenced without being tried; and often executed without evidence. It all depended upon the whim of the earl, or the baron, or bishop, or king, or what-not. But very gradually there was developed in England a genuine equality before the law, as may be traced through the following important watermarks of the evolution of the freedom of English-people: 1. Magna Charta; 2. The petition of Rights, 1628; 3. Habeas Corpus, 1679. In our Colonial days these gains made by the people of England naturally were enjoyed by the early settlers and they at last, after writing a Declaration of Independence, incorporated basic equality before the law in the Constitution, and in the first seven or eight amendments thereto.

As may be expected, equality before the law is not yet a realized fact for all. The lawyer for a great corporation told me that his employers were so powerful through their wealth that he would guarantee to keep any case indefinitely in the courts, and thus wear out any adversary, however just might be that man's claims. "The law's delays," is often a sad calamity for a poor man. In my own old home community I knew of two men whose opposite experiences illustrate this unfortunate fact. One was the president of a great corporation who in a federal court was found guilty on ten serious counts, but being a corporation president, and very wealthy, and very prominent, he paid not a cent of fine and did not spend a day in jail. When he returned to his home city he was met at the depot by a band and a long procession. The other man about whom I knew was a poor fellow who stole a coil of copper wire from a car-barn in the same city and served two years in the penitentiary for so doing! The reader knows of such cases, I have no doubt, and so does everybody. But this is only to say that any right which humanity gains is always imperfectly held and must be evermore completely won, and that every right must evermore be carefully guarded, for the whole tendency of human society, if men relax their vigilance, is to slide backwards. Equality before the law as we now enjoy it in this country is found nowhere else in the world save in England, France, and a few other nations. In the great portion of the world it is a thing unknown. If that equality is not yet a perfect thing, the challenge is to us; it is no sense a proof that the doctrine of equality is an impossible thing.

Can you narrate the history of the winning of such political equality as we know have? What is political equality? Do you have equality before the law ? Do you have it as much as the Standard Oil Company? What should be done about "the law's delays"? Does not the man who can hire a good law firm stand a better chance than the poor man who cannot hire a lawyer at all? Is that right? What can be done about it?

What holds true of equality before the law holds true of equality in every right and just sense. And we Masons are under a peculiar obligation to devote ourselves to the task of making equality everywhere a fact. For equality is one of our central tenets. The Fraternity never permits us to forget that; the ritual impresses it upon the candidate in every way; the lodge is so organized that everyone "meets upon the level." The candidate is made to feel that without the assistance of his fellows he is a poor, naked, blind, destitute thing without hope: the member is made to know that every Mason has the Masonic rights equal to every other Mason, and pays the same dues, enters on the same conditions, holds office on the same terms, and shares equally with all others the burdens and obligations of the Order.

Tell what you can about Masonic equality. How long has Masonry taught the doctrine? How much equality is there in the lodge room? Why is it the duty of Masons to enforce equality everywhere?

PART IX
LIBERTY

LORD ACTON, who was one of the most learned men of all times, one of the greatest scholars of the last century, and who left behind him as his monument the great *Cambridge Modern History*, had as his life work the task of writing a *History of Liberty*. On this he toiled for years, with two large houses full of books, with all manner of original materials in several languages, until he had accumulated great heaps of data. But alas! he never arrived at the point where he felt that he knew enough about liberty to write its history! and he died with all his knowledge in him, his magnum opus unwritten! Such an experience reminds us what a subject we have before us in the present work; how difficult it is to deal with; how little has as yet been really thought out about it; how scanty are men's experiences of it; and consequently how modest must be our own attempts in the present connection.

Before entering into a discussion of the subject, fashion in your own mind as definitely as you can what you mean by liberty, and what you mean by liberty as a Masonic teaching.

On the surface it might appear to some that Masonry in itself has not much liberty to give its own children. The initiate finds himself forced to rehearse a Ritual no single syllable of which can be changed; he is in the hands of a group of men who govern him and his fellow members; the subordinate lodge, as its very name implies, must adjust itself to the will of Grand Lodge: and the whole field covered by the Fraternity is hedged about by a series of Landmarks which, like the laws of the Medes and the Persians, change not. Where the individual finds himself so circumscribed, and compelled to move in so narrow a channel, how, say many, can he be said to have liberty?

Those who ask such a question betray the misunderstanding under which so many labor as regards what is and what is not liberty. They have a vague notion as to what it is, and they dimly feel that in some way there isn't much liberty to be had anywhere, either in institutions or in government, or in the way the world is made. If it chances that one of us has similar misgivings and doubts it may be worth while just here to examine two or three of the false conceptions of liberty which are so common.

Liberty is not merely freedom from restraint. How many there are who think it to be so! A friend who has spent many years in working among immigrants told me that hordes of aliens come in from southeastern Europe, and used to come in from Russia, who have been told over and over that in America there are no laws, no governments, no penitentiaries and fines, and that here every man may do as he pleases with no other man to hinder. Finding themselves so completely disillusioned when they discover the real truth about the nation, they grow sullen and rebellious, consider themselves cheated, and fall an easy victim to the fallacies of anarchy. Such ideas of liberty are born of fancy, for there is no part of the human race anywhere that does have, or ever has had, any experience of such a state. On the contrary every one of us knows from his own experiences that liberty and restraint go together and are in no sense necessarily opposed one to the other. In a family there is all manner of restraint needed, not only for the children but for the parents as well, who are unable to do a hundred things because there are children to care for at home; but even so, father, mother, and the children may all enjoy to the utmost the fullest family liberty. And we know that it is the same with a man's work. If he is running a farm he is compelled to remain at his post to care for his stock often when he would prefer to be elsewhere; that he must be up with the sun, and do a certain amount of plowing, harrowing, planting, harvesting, and what not, even though his fancies would lead him to do something very different. He has restraints enough, nevertheless he enjoys on his farm absolute liberty of toil, for the two things go together. And so it is in every kind of labor, and in every other sphere in which men live; always there are the fences about one, and the sign set up, "thus far shalt thou go but no farther," but that does not destroy liberty, which is a very different thing than freedom from restraint.

Nor is liberty the same as a go-as-you-please individualism. A large and powerful group of men in the last century taught that all things that check the individual are wrong, and that the full enjoyment of life comes only when the individual can consider himself a separate entity cut off from other individuals whom he is not to hinder and who are not to hinder him. The state is to have no right to interfere with the lives of men in any way, shape or form. Herbert Spencer, who may be considered typical of this school of thought, resented it when the state interposed to regulate education; when it undertook to levy income taxes and to direct business developments; he was bitter even against the governmental building of highroads which he believed should be left to the citizens in each given community. It may be true that such a conception of individualism would accord well with liberty, and it might be desirable, but unfortunately the experience of the nations has shown it utterly impossible of operation; it is not in harmony with the way men are made. Human nature is against it. For each individual man is by his very nature a social being who can no more be cut off from the social organization than a leaf can be safely cut from the branch of the parent tree. There are some things that we can do separately as private souls; there are other equally important things that we can do only as citizens of a community, as members of a social order. What would have become of us, to cite one example, if it had been left to individual enterprise to manage a war? In many, many cases the individual, for his own joy and welfare, must be held to his place in the social organism and made to perform his functions there.

Closely akin to the philosophical doctrine of individualism preached by Spencer are the theories of the "laissez faire" school of economics which played so large a part in the history of the nineteenth century. The members of this school believed that the business relations of men are governed by certain "economic laws" which operate in the same way as, and are as unchangeable as, the so-called laws of nature. Men must be left alone, was their cry, and not tampered with; hands off, and business will run itself; the world will be fed, clothed, and housed as automatically as the sun rises and sets. The chief of these "economic laws" was believed to be unfettered competition, indeed, competition was set up as such an important god that when, during the Irish famine in 1825 it was proposed to organize relief in England and ship corn to the starving millions many "economists" fought the project on the ground that the situation would be cared for by the normal functionings of the law of supply and demand and that nobody had any right to divert ships from the normal channels of trade. The theories of the "laissez faire" school seem quaint and far off to one at this date, for their whole scheme of thought has gone by the board, and that for a hundred reasons, one of which is that there are in economic life no such "laws" as those that operate in nature, and that such laws as do operate in economics are of the same kind as those that we find in all forms of human association; they are full of the action of men's wills, and desires, and deliberate planning. "To let things alone," to let things drift, does not mean that things will be cared for by automatic natural laws, but that the most predatory individuals in the community will use such a state as an opportunity to rob their fellows right and left. In our own government we have learned that business, in all its forms, is something that must be regulated like all other human activities, and that any ideal of liberty which assumes itself to consist of an absence of regulation is a false ideal.

All these various false notions of liberty have in common one thought, that it is a desirable thing to leave each individual to himself, uncontrolled by others; to let him be an entity in a void. Such a thought is false and impossible. Man is by his very structure a social being, and therefore one that must live, for the sake of his own happiness as much as for the sake of the happiness of others, ringed about by all manner of governing forces and influence.

In what way is liberty exemplified and taught in the Fraternity? What is the difference - if there is a difference - between "liberty" and "freedom"? How many kinds of liberty can you name, such as, for example, civil, religious, personal, etc.? Do you believe that the individual Mason, under the present system of Masonic laws and usages, enjoys as much freedom as he deserves? Does the subordinate lodge have sufficient independence? How would you differentiate "independence" from "liberty"? What other common terms express the same general idea? What does the Bible teach about liberty? Masons fought on both sides of the Civil War. Was that inconsistent with Masonry? Albert Pike was an officer in the Confederate army. Was that inconsistent with what be teaches about liberty and freedom in Morals and Dogma? If so, in what way was it inconsistent?

What liberties do American citizens now actually enjoy? Does the man enjoy real liberty in work who has a boss over him, who must go and come at a certain time, and have all the conditions of labor regulated by others? What is the "right to work"? Is it the same as "liberty of toil" ? What is meant by individualism? Can you name any great "Individualists" in our own national history? Was Lincoln an Individualist? What countries in Europe give their citizens civil liberty? Religious liberty? Liberty of thought? What can you tell about Herbet Spencer? What did he write? Can you illustrate from American industrial and business history the theory of "laissez faire"? What about railways, public corporations, etc., as things went forty years ago? How would you explain the fallacy of the "let things drift" school?

What then is Liberty?

In my own conception of it, liberty means that everyone is to enjoy unhindered the full exercise of the normal functions and powers of his nature. This is an entirely different conception than that implied in the no-restraint theory, because man's nature cannot function normally in a void, or in a condition of pure individualism: the functions and powers of a man's nature, when rightly understood, imply and demand a social life, a community of lives in which each individual finds his true happiness in his right relations to other human beings. It will be better to permit this conception to define itself through a series of examples and illustrations.

One of the most important powers of a man's nature is his mind. If the man is to be happy, if his nature is to be healthy and unmutilated, he must be permitted to live in a social order where he has absolute right to use that mind unhindered by anything or anybody. The mind is so made that any interference with its normal functioning brings distress to the individual and disorder to human society. Every attempt to dictate to men how they shall use their minds has proved to be disastrous, as history so abundantly proves. One may recall Prince Metternich and the Peace of Vienna in 1815 when the masters of Europe ordained what men should think, speak, and read. That regime did not bring the uniformity of thought and peace of life which the masters expected; it brought quite the contrary, a fermentation of embittered men and women which led finally to the outbursts of 1848. It is a peculiar agony to have one's very brain in chains: men must rebel or at last surrender, to sink in the apathy and listlessness of the peasant and the serf.

In what does liberty of mind consist? In the right to use it normally, for the health and the good of all. It does not mean that an individual is free to make use of his mind without restraint or hindrance of any kind. The man who uses his intellect to perpetrate a fraud should be held in leash; when he exercises it in the manufacture and dissemination of lies it is time that he feel that he is not the only man who lives in the world. When a man is set free to think he is set free, not for intellectual license and anarchy which is at last the absence of thought, but to think according to those laws of thinking which are inherent in the mind itself. Therefore freedom of thought does not lead to anarchy and confusion but to harmony, for all facts exist in the system of nature, and all truth is in harmony with itself. When we Masons contend for the right of the free intellect we are contending for the right and healthful use of the intellect, the normal use of it; not for mere caprice.

What can you tell about the history of intellectual liberty in the United States? Did the early colonists enjoy much of it? Do we have complete intellectual liberty now? What would your neighbors do or say if you were to speak out openly just what you think about religion, polities, morality, etc.? Do you now practice freedom of thought, and free speech? If not, why not? Have you freedom of thought and speech in your Masonic lodge?

So also with the right to choose one's own work, which is also essential to a state of liberty. During the last centuries of the Roman Empire the collegiate system (the collegia were a kind of craft union) had hardened to such rigidity that what a man's father had done that also must he do; he was not even free to leave his own village without permission; he existed in a kind of industrial slavery. The same thing recurred, or almost the same thing, at the end of the guild system in England: men had at last to break the system because it was destroying, the right of free work. In India, or in certain parts of it, the caste system functioned in the same manner to deprive the individual of the light to choose his own form of labor.

This right also exists in the very structure of man's nature. Each of us has his own "bent," and prefers his own "line." One man loves manual toil; another would be a musician; a third finds himself made to be a scholar. So goes it with all. This urge within one's nature toward a certain form of labor is as essential to manhood as the freedom of thought, and it is always as disastrous to human happiness when the freedom to work is denied as it is when men are deprived of freedom of mind. In any social order rightly conceived the liberty of every man to work as he chooses is essential.

But this does not mean that a man can exercise his desire unrestrained. It does not mean that an individual can do what he pleases as if he were alone in a void where no other man could be. It means that the right to work, like all other rights, is shaped by the structure of human nature, and by the necessities of society. If a given form of business proves destructive of social order, such for example as the business of war, or opium smuggling, or piracy, etc., then the man's right ceases. What we all should strive to uphold is the normal exercise of such rights.

As much may be said of the right of free worship, or liberty of religion. Religion is, it seems, an integral part of nature, therefore it must have healthy development else it lead to ills and to unhappiness. Interference with religious liberty, the long and dark attempts to dictate to men what and how they shall worship, has every time bred misery and degradation. A normal religiousness makes for the welfare of a man's life, and he therefore has a right to the free and normal exercise of it.

The same may be said of all the other functions and powers of our nature. We have an inherent right to choose our friends; to have a voice in our own government; to live where we desire; etc., etc. In all the possible forms which liberty may take we find this same truth, that this liberty is for the sake of the healthful exercise of human nature, so that a man can be happy while he lives, and that any interference with the normal functionings of the same leads to unhappiness, to the mutilation of nature, and is therefore a thing to be opposed and destroyed. And all this does not lead to individualism, to atomism, to any form of license, or to anarchy as many conservative minds fear, because if the functions of man's nature are rightly exercised, exercised according to human nature itself, freedom will not lead to conflict among men, but rather to unity and harmony. The very way in which a man is made causes him to be a part of nature, a part of society, and in constant relationship with God. Any liberty which divorces him from nature, or makes him an anti-social being, or causes him to violate the deep laws of his own spirit, is not real liberty at all, but its counterfeit.

Liberty, it follows from all that has been heretofore said, is therefore not a mere gift which the powers that be may confer on a man at their pleasure: it is called for by the very structure of man. It is something necessary, something demanded by the nature of things. Therefore it is, as our Declaration of Independence defined it, a natural right. It is a right that existed before governments came into existence; nay, governments exist in order to make it possible, and to preserve it inviolate. For law, lightly understood, exists in order that liberty may be unharmed.

When we have reached this conception we can no longer believe that such a thing can be a mere matter of simple instinct to any individual which he will straightway begin rightly to exercise the moment he is set loose to do as he pleases. Liberty, just because it is so deep and many-sided a thing, and sends so many roots down into human nature and so many ramifications out into human society, is a thing that must be learned. The baby chick has an instinct which teaches it how to eat the moment it steps out of the shell; some have held the theory that man has a similar instinct for liberty which he will exercise if only priests, kings, and aristocrats will let him be. Such a notion is a fallacy. We each one have the right to be free; but to be indeed free, that means a right education for the purpose. Freedom as a right exists in every man: freedom as a fact exists only in those natures which have prepared themselves for it.

Do we now have "liberty of work" in our present factory system? Can you tell a little about the history of religious liberty in this nation? Have we all always enjoyed it? How was it won? How many other nations are now fighting for religious liberty? What is the difference between spiritual, and religious, liberty, if any? Do bad habits hold a man in spiritual slavery?

From one point of view the whole of Masonry exists in order to teach men how to make right use of their prerogatives of freedom. The candidate is made to feel that he is not a separate living atom living and dying unto himself, but that he is by nature a part of a great brotherhood of men and women; he is taught that until he can exercise the powers of maturity he must, like all good apprentices, be content to have others lead him; he is made to understand that mature life is not his at a grasp, but that he lives in darkness concerning it until he has gone the whole road of preparation; he is shown that the hoodwink cannot be removed until he is duly obligated to his fellows and taught his duties; he is made to understand that unless he is able to walk alone and exercise his rights normally a cable-tow of external authority is needed to hold him in place, and that such a cable-tow must remain, about him until he is able to stand on his own feet; he is made to understand the ever present need of light, and that unless he is always seeking it, darkness will settle upon him, and darkness means unhappiness; and not until he is instructed how to be the absolute master of himself is he raised from the dead level of his slavery to the living perpendicular of a free man.

In its mysteries of initiation Freemasonry reveals itself to its adepts, under one of its aspects at least, as the preparation for the liberty of the mind, of the body, of the soul, of manhood and womanhood. Its part out in the great world among other powers and institutions also reveals it as the champion of liberty in all its forms and under all its veils. And it has ever contended for liberty because it has struggled to win for men life, more life, and life more abundantly. That is its mission. And because man needs liberty in order to richly live, it has striven to win liberty in all its forms. During the last hundred years Masonry has not been absent from one single struggle for civil, or political, or religious liberty. When men have sought to throw off the yoke of unlawful or cruel rulers it has lent them its aid. When they have prayed and bled to be relieved of the yoke of spiritual and religious bondage it has given them of its strength and made their war its own. Until man has won for himself all those freedoms wherein his life consists it will ever be so, because Masonry exists in order that we all may live more happily, more completely, more abundantly.

How do parents teach their children how to exercise freedom? How is it true that the law is for the sake of liberty? How many ways are there that Masonry teaches men, and drills men, and shapes men, to know what liberty is, and to exercise right liberty? What part is Masonry now playing, here and abroad, in the liberating of men? In how many revolutions has Masonry played a part? Do you believe in revolutions? What is the difference between a right revolution and a wrong revolution? What is Masonry now doing in Mexico, Central America, and South America? Why is the Masonic ideal of liberty so opposed by the Roman Catholic Church? The greatest Masonic teacher of liberty has been Albert Pike; can you explain his conception of it? Have you ever read his "Morals and Dogma"? What does be therein teach about liberty? What branch of the Masonic Fraternity has had most to say about this subject? What is the difference between liberty and equality? Between liberty and democracy?

PART X
DEMOCRACY

WHEN in the course of human events the mass of people living in a nation learn how to live together as a people, and devise means whereby to secure for themselves their rights as a people, and contrive political machinery and social institutions of such character as exist by and for the whole mass of individuals, that land may be said to be a democracy; for democracy may be described as a state of society in which the people as a whole control in their own collective interest the institutions and forces of the nation. No nation becomes democratic by first thinking out a theory of what democracy is and then, as an architect follows a blueprint, deliberately setting out to put the theory into practice; but they arrive at democracy very gradually and naturally, though not always without strife, by securing control of one thing and of another until they have control of everything, they then manage everything so as to satisfy the needs and desires of the people as a whole.

Some nations long for democracy, others are on the way to democracy, and others still may be said to possess it, albeit in no nation has it as yet become perfect. The most conspicuous among these last is, perhaps, our own country. It was the first great nation to adopt democracy wholeheartedly, and it has from the first never swerved from the path that leads to a more and more complete control of everything by the people themselves and in their own interests. Whether one should describe as democratic a nation that merely longs for it, or whether the name should be exclusively applied only to those nations which may be truly said already to possess it, must be left to the individual's opinion to decide. The use of words is one thing, facts are another. The organization of public life by and for the public - that is what we Americans strive for with all our hearts, unless we are renegades, and that is what we American Masons, with an equal whole-heartedness, believe the Masonic Fraternity to stand for.

How can a people ever be said to control their own life when always a minority, sometimes large, sometimes small, is opposed to the course of the majority? Is majority rule the same as democracy? Can you name a nation now existing which is trying to secure democracy? Name two nations now "on their way to democracy." What kind of a government did Alexander Hamilton wish us to have? What sort of a nation did Thomas Jefferson strive for? Were they both democrats? Do you believe that the mass of the citizenship of this nation is competent to manage its own affairs? A French writer (Fauget) describes democracy as "the cult of inefficiency." Do you agree with him? Or do you agree with President-Emeritus Eliot of Harvard University that democracy is the most efficient of governments ?

Now it is self evident that there may be many means whereby the public as a public may come into control of its own social forces and institutions. How democracy is to be won and preserved is a question of political and social machinery, and that is a question that cannot concern us here because it belongs to politics. Suffice to say that it is possible for the people directly to manage their own institutions, as in some cities the price of a bus ride is determined by popular ballot, which is usually described as "direct democracy," and that it is also possible for the people to control their own institutions through elected representatives as is usually done among us, which method is called the "republican" or "representative" system. In our own nation we mix up the two methods very much and the United States might be properly described as a democracy in the form of a republic.

What is meant by political science? What is sociology? What is economics? Give examples from your own knowledge of "direct democracy." Of "representative democracy." Can you explain the difference between the Democratic Party and the Republican Party on this question?

Some may have been wondering why it should be necessary to include in this little book a section on democracy when the course includes two other papers on equality and liberty respectively. Well, it may be said in reply that while democracy includes equality and liberty, equality and liberty may exist without democracy, and that in our nation, and also I believe in our Fraternity, we strive for all three together. Liberty means that a man is free to develop and use the functions of his own nature without undue interference from others. Equality means that one man has the same fundamental nature as another man, and should have the same privileges to live; but it has often happened that a social structure has existed in which only a minority of the people have been permitted to enjoy either liberty or equality. In Athens, for example, a fraction of the populace was composed of citizens enjoying liberty while the great bulk of them were slaves, and in many parts of India, to cite an example of the other kind, all the individuals enjoy liberty but, owing to a very hard-and-fast caste system, they do not have equality. The democrat (this must not be confused with the member of the political party which employs that name) believes that liberty is a good thing for each individual and that therefore a state should guarantee it to all, and he also thinks that the state should provide genuine equality for all. A state in which all the social forces and values are controlled by and for all the people, and which is so organized at the same time as to guarantee for all liberty and equality, may be thought of as the ideal toward which all true democrats are working. If it be true, as I think it is true, that Freemasonry is one of the mightiest forces working in that direction, we may all feel that no institution could be of more value to our nation than Freemasonry.

We must be careful not to conceive of democracy being merely political. I should advance this as a criticism of James Bryce's definition in his treatise, already seen to be a great work, called "Modern Democracies." He says that "Democracy really means nothing more nor less than the rule of the whole people expressing their sovereign will by their votes." That is clearly a merely political definition. Democracy is oft something besides a "rule": it may be an expression of the popular life, as in what we call democratic art, like the "Leaves of Grass" by Walt Whitman; and when it is a rule it may be exercised in quite other ways, as when social changes are brought about or prevented by the power of public opinion; and also it often happens that the mere unconscious growth and changing of a people may transform important conditions in a nation's life.

Then, too, I think one should quarrel with Viscount Bryce's definition in that it ignores such things as social democracy, industrial democracy, and intellectual democracy. By social democracy we mean that social customs and conditions should be controlled and shaped by all the people in the interests of all the people. By industrial democracy we mean that industry shall be controlled by and in the interests of everybody; and by intellectual democracy we mean that there shall be no mere caste of thinkers as there was in Ancient Egypt but that everybody will use his brains and that science and scholarship exist for all and by all. The organizing of science and scholarship in public schools which function under the control of the state is an example of how the intellectual life may become genuinely democratic. How all these things may be accomplished or perfected is a question of ways and means, and belongs to those discussions in which we strive to discover what are the most perfect social mechanisms, and therefore do not come within our present province.

It is wise for us to learn to look at the facts themselves, and do our own thinking by means of them, rather than to let ourselves be deceived by words. For oftentimes it happens that a nation may call itself a democracy or a republic and yet have not even a tithe of the reality for which these names stand. Mexico under Diaz may have had a very stable government but it was not a democracy, though Diaz and his grandees were careful to observe the formalities, and carried on "elections" every once in a while. Diaz called himself a "President" but in reality was a dictator. In England, on the other hand, there is a king and a royal house but everybody knows that the English people are quite as democratic as we are, because their great governing body is immediately responsible to the people, and is elected directly by the people.

Can you tell in what ways some of our own social institutions are not yet democratic? What is a social institution? Name five. Do you believe that industry should be socialized, or brought under public control? Is this the same as Socialism? If not, in what way does it differ? How could industrial democracy be brought about? Can you name any country that calls itself a democracy which is really not? Name a democratic country that still has a king but is really democratic. Is Belgium a democracy?

It may be safely said that Freemasonry is about the most democratic institution in existence. On its lodge floor men of all grades of rank, wealth and influence meet together in absolute equality, so that Presidents of the United States have sat on the side lines while some humble workman governed in the East. Its members are elected by secret ballot; its officers are chosen by ballot also; and it is governed by laws administered through representatives who must, once a year, give an account of their trust to the body of the membership. It is so organized that its responsibilities and privileges are equally distributed among the whole membership so that all share equally.

The democratic nature of the Craft is shown by its actual conduct in history during the past two hundred years. It arose in England (I refer here to modern speculative Masonry as we now know it) when society in general hated and loathed the idea of democracy, and when men were broken up into social classes of such rigidity as really to constitute genuine castes; but in its lodges it gave to every man absolute freedom of thought and expression and it put into practice those methods of popular rule which we have now in our government. Since its reorganization in 1717 it has always thrown its weight, or at least with very few exceptions if any, on the side of popular rule. I had occasion recently to read every reference to Freemasonry in the Encyclopedia Britannica, and I was struck by the fact again and again that the Fraternity received mention almost every time as being one of the forces on the side of a revolt against tyranny in some country, as, for example, in Spain and in Belgium. We know how that a great many of the founders of our nation were active members of the Craft; how that the Declaration of Independence has been freely described, even by the profane, as a Masonic document; and how it can be accurately said that the Constitution of the United States is Masonry put into political practice; and we also know that Masons were very active in tormenting and carrying through the American Revolution. My friend and colleague, Cyrus Field Willard, of San Diego, California, has prepared a paper on "The Origin of the Scottish Rite", in which he shows that European Jews of great wealth were so anxious to see organized here a democracy in which they could have full citizenship and never be in danger of persecution that they poured vast sums of money into the coffers of the Revolutionary government; and that they made use of lodges, and organized many such, in order to carry on their work through Masonry.

The teachings and principles of Freemasonry can never be realized in any state of society save a democratic one. How could there be equality for all in a nation ruled by a class, or a caste, or a clique of bureaucrats, or a set of multi-millionaires? How could liberty be guaranteed to every last man in a nation that did not govern itself through laws that apply equally to all, and are interpreted and executed by men chosen by the people and responsible to the people? In any other kind of government liberty and equality may be granted for a time as a privilege but there is never any way of knowing, as history itself so abundantly attests, when that privilege will be withdrawn.

The foregoing mention of the Scottish Rite reminds one of Masonry's great book, Albert Pike's "Morals and Dogma." Those who have carefully read that wonderful work ("those" should include every Mason, whether he be a member of the Scottish Rite Bodies or not) will recall how that liberty and equality sound through its pages over and over like a mighty bell, and how that the author interprets the whole of history as a vast conflict between the forces that make for tyranny and the forces that make for freedom. It is often asked why Scottish Rite Masonry makes such headway in Latin countries where Ancient York Masonry stagnates: I believe the reply to be this, that Albert Pike and the founders of the Scottish Rite System organized a Masonry that may be readily translated into a people's yearning for political freedom. They read in its mighty palimpsest their own prayers for liberation; they find in it a power for emancipation; it is an irresistible force for the overthrow of thrones and dominions.

But is must not be supposed that Freemasonry works for democracy only when it is engaged in some actual struggle, as it was during our Revolutionary period. Its silent and perpetual influences, quiet as the coming of the night, unostentatiously prepare in every Masons mind those thoughts and feelings which make toward democracy. It has become a commonplace with political thinkers that democracy cannot come to any people until they have prepared themselves for it. It is not a magic that acts independently of the citizenship; it is a thing that people themselves do if it be done, and it cannot be unless they learn how to do it, and until they desire it with a ceaseless desire. A great Order of more than two and one-half million members in this nation exercises an immeasurable influence toward a full and complete democracy by constantly instilling into its members those ideas and longings which inwardly prepare them for the fullest measures of equality and liberty. As the sun works so potently in the spring in developing the young seeds until a luxuriant vegetation breaks forth, so does the mighty Order that is dedicated to Light throw its fructifying warmth about the mind and heart of everyone of its children. And it does this ceaselessly. It knows no seasons: it has no winter.

Democracy, I said, is not a kind of magic that works whether or no. It is not an infallibility. When the people govern themselves they do not escape mistakes nor are they miraculously freed from weaknesses and evils. The theory of democracy is that the people can learn to govern themselves only by governing themselves, just as an individual learns by experience and experiments. Therefore though the people, or let us say "we," may fail, time and again, that is no reason for despairing of democracy.

In the foregoing section are mentioned a few ways in which Freemasonry is democratic; can you name others? Can you give examples of how Freemasonry has actually fought on the side of political liberty? Why can't a democratic institution like ours flourish in an undemocratic society? What is the principal idea in Pike's "Morals and Dogma"? What does that name mean? Has Freemasonry made you more democratic? How can one carry out the ideals of democracy in every day conduct? How would you change Masonry to make it more democratic? Could it be made more democratic?

PART XI
MASONRY AND INDUSTRY

OUR MODERN industrial system dates back to 1789 in which year James Watt successfully, demonstrated the feasibility of the power machine for industrial purposes. Prior to that time almost all work, as the name "manufacture" (which means "make by hand") itself indicates, was carried out by hand. Tools were simple and inexpensive, and there was little necessity for great factory buildings and no possibility of manufacturing cities such as are now so familiar to us. The worker was closer to his work, and felt more interest in it, and had more at stake in it, and often he himself purchased the raw materials in which he worked, and owned the tools whereby he transformed raw products into articles of commerce.

The introduction of the steam engine, and other power machines, changed all that. The machine was too expensive for the workman to own; it had to be housed in special buildings (factories) designed for it; using such large quantities of stuff and turning out such immense quantities of finished products it was necessary to devise the railroad in order to tend it. The dependence of one kind of manufacturing upon another led manufacturers to herd together at convenient centers and thus the industrial city came into existence. Things could be made that were never made before, and a hitherto undreamed of quantity of new wealth came into existence. Under this regime workmen could no longer own their own tools but became employees, selling their labor in the market as a commodity. The machinery of production passed into the hands of wealthy men, and as a consequence we have the present divisions of society so familiar to us all: the group owning and controlling the raw materials of production and the machinery of manufacture and distribution; the group made up of industrial laborers; and the large class of small merchants and professional men who cater to the needs of these two groups.

It would be easy for any economist (the writer makes no claim to any such dignity) to quarrel with this picture, but the picture may stand for all that as a not inaccurate description of the way things are, and of how they came so to be. At any rate, it will serve to introduce us to the points worthy of discussion in the present study.

How would you describe the industrial system that existed before 1789? Who was James Watt? What great invention did he make? How has the power changed the whole face of the earth, and brought about a complete reconstruction of human society? Name the ten basic industries. What is meant by an "industrial system"? How did our large cities arise? What is the importance of transportation systems in modern life? What is meant by "economist"? Have you ever fashioned for yourself a theory of Freemasonry's attitude toward industrial problems?

Inasmuch as this great industrial system produces such an immense quantity of wealth we very naturally find a great deal of rather earnest rivalry among the various industrial groups who, each one, strive to capture as large a share of it as possible. Accordingly, we find capitalists, proprietors, merchants, etc., forming corporations, associations, and so forth, as a means of securing their stake in the system; and at the same time laboring men form unions, farmers have their granges, and professional and mercantile groups build up all manner of systems, and all this in nearly every case in order to secure or to protect a certain interest in the values being produced daily by the industrial system.

This conflict of groups due to their often conflicting group interests has come to be familiarly known to us in these days as "the class struggle." Oftentimes men talk of the class struggle as if it were a new invention, something only recently come into existence, but as a matter of fact, as Professor Franklin H. Giddings has been pointing out in a series of lectures, the class struggle is as old as war, and has played in all history quite as conspicuous a part as it does now though it was never quite so much to the front in discussion as it is now.

The various ways of describing and explaining and interpreting this class struggle, and the forces that have brought it about and of the manner in which its problems may be solved, have caused men to fall into a variety of different groups of thought or theory. The Anarchist believes that the industrial system is all as it now exists because it has so powerfully strengthened the hands of government, and therefore multiplied the opportunities of political tyranny, a thing he dreads more than he dreads the plague. The Communist would like to see the ownership of the raw materials, the machinery of production, and of the systems of distributions vested in the hands of the masses of the common people, without distinction of intellectual ability, wealth, or any such thing. The Socialist would like to see the industrial system owned and managed by the people at large in such wise that workers would produce only for use and not for profit, and each worker would receive just what he produces, no more and no less. The Guild Socialist would welcome a return of the old guilds whereby a given industry would be managed jointly by all the members engaged in it, with more emphasis on the social and artistic side of labor, and less emphasis on the money side of it. The Syndicalist would like to see all the members of each of the great industries own that industry in such wise that all the industries could be associated together in a general system, which general industrial system would fulfill all the functions now filled by our political governments. The Capitalist, or the man who takes the position which may be thus described, believes that the present system is the only fair and possible method of making the goods needed by the world. The Christian Socialist believes that if the teachings of Christianity were consistently applied to the industrial system it would result in a Socialist state, but that the ordinary Socialistic methods of arriving at such an end are quite wrong; in other words, it trusts in moral suasion rather than in industrial war or the class struggle.

From another point of view all these groups fall into only two groups, which may be described as Revolutionary or Reformist. In the latter case a man believes that the industrial system as it now exists is sane and sound but that there are details and conditions in it here and there that badly need changing, and he is in favor of making these reforms but refuses to touch the system as a whole. On the other hand the revolutionary is now concerned in mere local abuses or failures in the system: he is convinced that the system as a whole is wrong, and he works to uproot the system entirely in order utterly to destroy it so as to replace it by something entirely different. Revolutionaries again could be divided into classes, were there any need in the present instance, because some of them desire one kind of a system and some another, and some believe that the change could be made in one manner while others believe that it can only be made in other ways.

To illustrate... If a man believes that coal miners do not receive adequate wages he may work to increase their pay and would accordingly be classed as a reformer. If he believed that it is utterly wrong for coal mines to be owned and managed by individuals and for coal miners to be wage workers selling their labor as a commodity, and if he strives to bring about a regime wherein coal mines will be owned in some social way, he is a revolutionary. If he resorts to guns in order to bring this change about he is in favor of violence: if he thinks he can bring it about by peaceable means he will not believe in violence but will be a revolutionary nevertheless. In that instance the Communist would say, Let us all, without distinction, own and run the coal mines together. The Syndicalist would say, Let the coal miners own and run the mines for their own sakes. The Political Socialist would say, Let the people own the mines, and let them through some kind of popularly controlled government own and manage these mines, and let coal be produced as we need it, and nobody make a profit out of it.

One might name a score of other groups, such as the Single Taxers, the Land Nationalists, the Cooperationists, etc., but there is no need to multiply instances, especially since this is not an essay in economics but in Masonry. Masonry, as such, does not take sides with any of these groups. Its members may be doubtless found among them all, for in Europe there are many Masons who may belong to some one of the various Socialist or other radical groups, and in this country there are trade unionists, capitalists, etc., etc., everywhere in our lodges. But that makes no difference to these men as Masons, because as Masons they thrust these differences aside: also, as it is laid down in Masonic law, politics and kindred subjects are not discussed in lodge. Therefore it is perfectly plain that Masonry has nothing to do with these conflicting industrial and political groups as such. But - and here is the whole point of the present study - the Fraternity nevertheless has very much at stake in the present industrial conflicts, for industry occupies so large a place in the foreground of individual and social life, and exercises so potent an influence over everything we are or do, that the fortunes of a great national fraternity like ours are very much bound up with the fortunes and issues of the industrial system.

Can you give an example of the class struggle drawn from ancient history? From medieval history? What is meant by "class struggle"? Give evidences of its existence drawn from your own observations. Has Anarchy ever had control of a people? Name a few of the more famous Anarchists. What is the difference between Communism and Socialism? What can you tell about Karl Marx and his theories? Did you ever read "The Communist Manifesto" by Marx and Engles? What did Marx teach in his "Capital"? Are there any guilds now in existence? What would the Syndicalists do with our own government if they could get hold of it? Can you name any prominent Syndicalists? Do the Capitalists have organizations similar to trade unions ? If so, what are they, and what do you think of them? What should be the attitude of Freemasonry toward trade unionism? What can you tell about Christian Socialism? Can you describe and define the Cooperative movement, not mentioned in the paper? Do you believe we need a new industrial system? Or do you think the present system is sound? What is meant by Land Nationalization? How would that affect an industrial system? Would you admit an Anarchist to membership in the Fraternity? Do you know any Masons who are Socialists? Just what, according to your own views, does Freemasonry have at stake in the present industrial system? What is the attitude of French Masonry toward the industrial crisis? Of English Masonry?

Freemasonry strives to make all men brethren, living amicably and happily together; if an industrial system is such as to divide men into quarrelling factions, sometimes making actual war on each other, it is manifest that the aims of the Fraternity are defeated by the evils in the industrial system. Freemasonry looks toward universal peace said international cooperation: if industrial methods and interests, as exemplified in tariffs and large foreign investments, drive nations apart and into some form of war, then Freemasonry, is thwarted. Freemasonry strives for equality but if an industrial regime is of such a nature as to divide society into castes and cliques, the members of which look with jealousy and suspicion upon each other, then it is clear that Freemasonry must suffer defeat. Whatever makes impossible the realization of the ideals of the Craft is in reality the enemy of Masonry, and will be opposed by genuine and living Masonry. Whatever makes it possible for Masonic ideals to be realized, will be supported and strengthened by Masonry.

In any discussion of the philosophy of industry, Freemasonry, if it remain true to its own philosophy, must take the position that industry exists for the sake of man, and must be so managed as to make for the welfare of man. What man is, and what man needs, and what will make it possible for man to live a normal and happy life, that is the criterion by which an industrial system is to be judged.

If we men and women are to remain alive, and if we are to live lives of reasonable happiness, then certain things are necessary to us, such as food, clothing, fuel, houses, education, amusement, and all that. Industry is the method which we have devised whereby these wants and needs may be satisfied. If at any point, or in any moment, the industrial system is failing to satisfy these needs then that industrial system is a failure and must be reorganized. I have to work in order to live but if no work is to be had, something is radically and dangerously wrong. I need clothing, but if, whatever be my efforts, I cannot get clothing, I am forced to rebel against the way things are. I have to find food in order to remain alive, but if there is no food to be had, it is manifest that there is a breakdown somewhere. To say that an industrial system is a thing that has come about through some mechanical process of mature, like the fall of rain, and that therefore we must passively endure its evils as well as enjoy its goods, is a very foolish way of thinking, because an industrial system is a very human thing, a thing we have brought into existence, a thing over which we always have, if we will but exercise it, a great deal of control. This, however, is not to imply that the present system is wrong; far from it; the point I make is that the one possible criterion whereby to test a system is the question, How successfully does it minister to human needs? The question as to the success or shortcomings of the system now at work is quite irrelevant in the present connection, and must be left to the economists and the industrial experts.

What effect does the present industrial system have on brotherhood, international relations, peace, equality? What does an industrial system exist to do? Is our present system fulfilling the functions which we have a right to ask of it? Are you able, through honest effort, to secure sufficient work, food, clothing, fuel, etc.? What effects do the possession of great private fortunes have upon a nation? What is meant by industrial democracy ?

In connection with the above it must also be noted that one should not make impossible demands of an industrial system, as is too often the fashion of zealous but inexperienced reformers. There are many things in nature that cannot be changed, and we must adjust our industrial systems to those things. I may not like to mine coal in the damp galleries underground, but that is where coal is to be found, so I must make the best of it. I may not enjoy living in the far north where the winters are so long and cold, but if I am to have pine lumber that is where I must go to get it. The sea is too often a damp and cheerless place in which to live, but if I need fish I must go to sea to get them. Many of the conditions under which we have to work may be uncomfortable and even dangerous, but such conditions must not be charged up against the industrial system if these things cannot be changed. Also, it should be remembered that there is no magic in industry: if a given quantity of goods are to be produced, then a certain amount of work is required to produce it, and that means that man will be compelled to work so many hours, so that it may sometimes happen that a work day will have to be long. And there is a limit to the possibilities of tools, instruments, and inventions, so that often it will necessarily be a hard and dangerous thing to do certain kinds of work, no matter how much improvement there may be by way of inventive genius. This is only another way of saying that while we insist that a given industrial system must satisfy the needs of human beings in a satisfactory manner we must take care not to frame that requirement in such wise as to make it impossible of realization: the fixed conditions of nature must be taken into consideration, the limitations of devices and tools, and the limitations in human power and human wisdom.

Give examples of impossible demands made on our industrial system by reformers. How do you judge the worth and desirability of any reform? By what standards do you judge industrial practices? How can you prove, for example, whether or not the eight-hour day should be put everywhere into practice ?

Freemasonry is wedded to high ideals, and insistent on lofty demands, but even so it is unwise of Masons to suppose that therefore it has any right to expect any sudden utopia. It does have a right, however, to ask that this world be made and kept a human world in which men can live together as brothers: and it should insist that the manner in which we make and distribute the goods of life should be of such a character as will make possible the realization of those fine and human goals toward which makes its way. For Masonry is itself a living organism and cannot live in a hostile environment.

In American Freemasonry we cannot discuss such things in our lodges, and it is probable that Masons will very seldomly as Masons care to discuss such matters outside of lodges. Be that as it may, if we are going to take our task seriously, and if we are sincerely in earnest to make right relations and brotherhood prevail we should all as individuals think out our industrial problems from the point of view of the Craft's own purposes and ideals. Nothing presses more closely upon us in these days, nothing is more fraught with the potentialities of great change and nothing will do more to reshape the world in which Freemasonry, like every other institution, must abide, than our industrial system and the burning problems which now beat about it. The Craft must find its own way through all this, and adjust itself to it, and do its own right part in it: how that can be, and when, and where, and to what results, all that is the problem of the Masonic philosophy of industry, a thing not yet born, but which must be born sooner or later.

What has Masonry a light to demand of an industrial system? Is Masonry actually making such demands? If so, how? How can such questions as these be studied by Masons as Masons? Should Masonic magazines discuss industrial problems? How is it possible to work out a Masonic Philosophy of Industry ?

PART XII
THE BROTHERHOOD OF MAN

OFTEN we hear it said by zealous reformers that we men must learn to be social beings, that individualism, egoism, and all such creeds are vicious in their effects, and-that the socializing of life will bring in an era of which William Morris dreamed when he wrote that "Brotherhood is heaven, the lack of brotherhood is hell." (Or did he use the word fellowship?" It matters not.) Admirable as is the spirit and intent of these reformers a fallacy lies at the heart of their theory. We men are already social beings: we were born that way. To tell us that we must become social is like telling fish to live in the water.

When a human babe is born it finds itself from the first in the midst of a family, and bound by indissoluble ties to father, mother, brother, and sister. After the child grows up a little, it discovers itself to have neighbors all about it. When school years come he learns that there are hundreds of other little people like himself. After he has reached maturity he will marry and have a family of his own. If he engages in an occupation he will find, almost without an exception, that his daily work is made possible by the fact that there are the human beings to whom he is tied by all manner of common interests.

The social nature of man's world is reflected in the structure of his own body and mind. He is possessed of the faculty of speech, which implies that there are others about him who have something to communicate to him, and to whom he has something to communicate. Nearly all his thinking has reference to his relations with others. When he sets himself to the task of learning, most of his learning is about others, and what they have been or done. The very nature of his private self-consciousness, so the psychologists have learned, is such that if a babe could grow up alone on a desert island it would be idiotic or insane, no matter how healthy it might be in body. There is no way in which a man can set out to become a social being, because he is already a social being, and can never be anything else. Sociality is an organic fact, built into the nature of man and of man's world, from which a man can no more escape than he can escape from his skin. This fact, so it seems to me, is absolutely essential to a right understanding of our subject.

Give your own definition of "brotherhood." Carefully examine in your own mind the idea that man is by nature a social being. Give other facts than those in the second paragraph to prove that man is a social being by nature. What is the difference between "sociality" and "sociability"? What has the social nature of man to do with Freemasonry? Could Freemasonry succeed in its mission if it were true that man's nature is essentially egotistic and anti-social?

These facts are to us so self-evident that it seems impossible that any mature person could ever have overlooked them: such however has been the case, and that with millions, for this understanding of man as by nature a social being is one of the achievements of modern thinking and scientific research. Once psychologists assumed that man comes into existence as a lonely individual untied to others, and that he gradually assumed social relations. Sociologists and political economists were hard put to explain how a self-sufficient individuality like man ever came to exist in communities. Rousseau advanced the theory of the "Social Contract" as his explanation of the matter: Hobbes brought forth another theory, and so on. Economists began their treatises with an account of some hypothetical man living on a desert island and then tried to show how that man's economic interests would lead him to form industrial associations with others. The theologians placed before their minds a picture of an individual brought into existence as a solitary unit, who had later to be brought somehow into relation with God with man. All such theorizing, then or now, for it still lives in some form or other with many men, is useless because it begins by assuming that man is a solitary unit who must become social by his own effort, whereas the truth is that a man is a social being already, and from the very beginning.

This being true it is easily seen that brotherhood is anything but a merely sentimental aspiration, which sensitive people can feel, and idealistic people can strive after. On the contrary it is already a fact, as hard and real a fact as the mother rock that makes the foundation of the mountains. To practice brotherhood is to discover that we men are already brothers by nature and that we can never be happy, or live in harmony with the laws and forces of our own beings, until we learn to love each other, and to cultivate the fraternal spirit. Men make a fatal mistake who suppose that we are really by nature such beings as the wolf or the tiger, that we are kept from devouring each other only by fear or custom, and that he who builds on raw egotism is the only man who has Nature on his side. The only man who has Nature on his side is he who builds on the fact that man is a social being, and therefore that he can never be happy until he is in harmony with his fellows.

Can you furnish other examples of how much of the thinking of the past has assumed that man is by nature an unsocial being? In what sense is it true that "brotherhood" is already a fact? Were the French the brethren of the German, and vice versa, during the battle of Verdun? If they were not, when were they brothers? Are they brothers now? How can they become brothers, if not? Do you habitually act on the supposition that each man you know is by nature an egotistic being who must be coaxed into being social? Is unselfishness as natural as selfishness?

Our present day psychologists, who are making such careful investigations of instincts, tell us that the old idea that the first and most powerful force in a man is the instinct of self-preservation, and that everything else must be secondary to that, is a fearful fallacy. The truth is, so they aver, that the instincts which look towards others, such as the instinct of parenthood, and the instinct of sociality, are equally primitive and equally powerful, and that the individual who stultifies those instincts will suffer in a hundred ways. Why is it that a man who sees some person about to drown, and that one a total stranger, will dart away from his own wife and children to leap into the water to try and save them, and there risk possible death? He doesn't reason or argue about the matter, but acts on his instinct. The need to live a brotherly life is written in the very scriptures of blood and tissue and bone, and he who lives in opposition to that need will bring himself into an abnormal condition in which his happiness will perish. This, so it seems to me, is one of the first laws of brotherhood: it is no mere sentimental luxury, but a necessity, and that in the same sense that bread and air and water are necessities.

One may describe brotherhood as the normal development of the social instincts, or he may describe it as the wise, commonsense adjustment of one's self to one's fellows. When one makes that wise and harmonious adjustment he makes it not in response to some sentimental and pious wish that such things should be, but in response to facts, to the way things really are with man's being. Just as a man must be in right relation with the food he eats in order to maintain health, so must he likewise be in right relation to his fellows if he would live in happiness.

The man who understands that brotherhood is one form of wisdom, and that it is demanded by the way things really are in man's world, will not be troubled by sentimental difficulties. Neither will he permit a few accidental private experiences to sour him of all brotherly striving. It may be that my neighbor and I have natures that are the antipodes of each other. What I admire he detests. What he loves I hate. His temperament is antagonistic to mine. My vocation is one that is opposed to his interests. We cannot hold social intercourse because we discover too many antipathies. Such a thing has nothing to do with brotherhood when it is rightly understood. Brotherhood does not demand of us that we privately like people who are obnoxious to us, or that others should like us who find our company distasteful. Such things are in the domain of one's intimate likes and dislikes and have to do with private friendship rather than with brotherhood.

If I cannot like this neighbor of mine I can be a brother to him nevertheless. I can give him exact justice in all my dealings with him. I can always refuse to do evil to him or speak evil of him. I can always maintain an attitude of good will to him, and wish for him good fortune and happiness. I can ever stand ready to help him to fullness of life, insofar as circumstances make that possible, and I can always refuse to place any obstacles in his path. If I have a difference with him I can differ with him as one man to another, honestly and openly, without childish petulance. Such in attitude is the brotherly spirit, and it can flourish where private friendship is impossible.

Who are the "psychologists"? What are the various instincts at the bottom of man's nature? Is the instinct of fraternalism as deeply rooted as the instinct of self-preservation? How do you get along with persons you do not personally like? Does brotherhood demand that we have a personal liking for every man? Could such a thing be possible? What is meant by the saying in the V.S.L. that "We should love one another," and "Love your enemies"? How can a man "love" his enemies? How can one Mason love another Mason whom he personally dislikes?

Practical men of affairs usually like to think of brotherhood in the terms of cooperation, and that is perfectly legitimate. The greatest things in the world - it is a banal statement to make - are accomplished by a great many men agreeing to act harmoniously together. A good Masonic research society or club is an example of this. We who belong to groups, and work for them (this includes you as well as myself) have no desire (or opportunity) to make money out of it, or to gain private ends by means of it. We are all interested to learn and teach more about Freemasonry and we have therefore formed a societies whereby we may the better accomplish that purpose. Such a thing is in itself brotherhood. The great Quatuor Coronati Lodge of Research, founded in England in 1884 is a case in point. The able scholars who toiled so diligently under the aegis of the lodge, and who laid the whole Fraternity under such an obligation to them, toiled without money and without price, but solely in order that we could all know more about our Craft. In so doing those men acted as brothers in as literal a sense as if they had all donned monk's habits and gone to live somewhere in the communal society of a monastery.

Can you give two or three other examples of brotherhood as being cooperation? Could one describe the cooperation, or "team play," of a baseball club as being brotherhood? Do you believe in brotherhood sufficiently to practice it? to risk things on the strength of it?

In Freemasonry we speak of the bond which holds men together in such endeavor as the "Mystic Tie." It is quite impossible to describe or to explain that tie, those who know what it is by experience, do not need it to be defined. There is something of private friendship in it, for I believe that the majority of Masons have a feeling towards brother Masons that they do not have towards outsiders, and there is something of the purpose of cooperation in it, as described above. It is a mixture of these two things, plus many other things.

Be that as it may it is true that what we mean by that tie is really the hope of the world. It is only as men are bound by it, whether they are Masons or not, that the human race can go on towards happiness. For after all is said and done the world is a unity, and is one. That is the nature of mankind and mankind can never be happy in living until all act in harmony with their nature. Those who make sport of the aspirations towards racial unity, internationalism, all such endeavors to bind man closer to man, woman to woman, know not of what they speak though they know it not, it is they who are miss by sentimental illusions, and imaginary mirages, the men who work to build life on the foundations on which life was intended to rest.

In proportion as a man understands brotherhood and acts in conformity with its demands, he will always work for human unity. In his lodge he will not be a dividing and distracting force. In his community he will be a good citizen who knows that the community has a right to demand many sacrifices on the part of its children. He will uphold and maintain the principles of his country, and oppose every influence that makes for its degeneration and division. He will everywhere use his efforts to break down racial antipathy, religious differences, and class hatred. War, fanaticism, national jealousies and unjust ambitions, the base intrigues of false statesmen, and the public connivance in public vices, he will everywhere and oppose. It is his task as a true soldier of brotherhood.

Masonry has played a great part in bringing about these conditions, and the part it is yet to play "is more than the twelve labors of Hercules." It is a great thing for the world that at a time when everywhere the spirit of strife and division is so rampant there should be in existence a powerful international body of men who preach and emphasize the need for unity, harmony, and international comity. I like to think that the Fraternity is a kind of great school in which men learn brotherhood by practicing it towards fellow Masons, because he who begins by practicing it towards fellow Masons will come sooner or later to practice it everywhere. And I like to think that Freemasonry is a world inside the world, and that in Masonry those habits of fraternity are developing which will one day take root everywhere. While the winter winds are raging the gardener sows the seed in the protection of his hothouse. After a while the plants will be carried outdoors to live under the sky. Inside the protecting arms of the Fraternity is growing a spirit which, as rapidly as conditions permit, must make itself felt everywhere. The great work of the world must be done by the combined and cooperating efforts of all the men of the world. At present that world lies dismembered about us, bleeding at every pore. This does not mean that brotherhood is a failure. It means that a world without brotherhood is a failure. It is the only practicable means of healing the hurts of mankind. Every individual who learns in the lodge the lessons of brotherhood and who goes through life everywhere practicing that lesson is helping toward the new order of things wherein will dwell peace for all men.

A thing that must achieve such a work as this cannot be a puny growth of private sentimentality. It is a world power capable of gigantic efforts. Those who think of it merely as a hand clasp and a slap on the back are dealing with it like children. It is a world law, destined to change the earth into conformity with itself, and as a world power it is something superb and awe-inspiring.

I speak the password primeval, I give the sign of Democracy; By God! I will accept nothing which all cannot have their counterpart of on the same terms....

I dreamed in a dream
I saw a city invincible to the attacks of the whole of the rest of the earth;
I dreamed that was the new City of Friends;
nothing was greater there than the quality of robust love - it led the rest .....
Swiftly arose and spread around me the peace and ledge that pass all the argument of the earth,
And I know that the hand of God is the promise of my own,

And I know that the spirit of God is the brother of my own,
And that all men ever born are also my brothers and the women my sisters and lovers,
And that a kelson of the creation is love. . . .
Is it a dream?
Nay, but the lack of it the dream,
And, failing it, life's lore and wealth a dream,
And all the world a dream "
(Whitman.)

PART XIII
FREEMASONRY AND RELIGION

THE EARLY operative builders of the Middle Ages were churchmen, if we may trust the many histories of architecture which deal with the subject. This was especially true after the Gothic, or pointed arch, superseded the old Romanesque style with its round arch and its gloomy interiors, for the advent of the Gothic coincided with a revival of interest in church architecture. This revival reached such proportions of zeal and devotion that bishops themselves studied to become architects (that word was not in use then, but the function was) and raised such great sums of money for the purpose that many little towns erected cathedral structures that would now be pointed to with pride by our great rich modern cities. Needless to say, these builders, the bishop directors and overseers along with the men who did the toil, were true and loyal sons of the Roman Catholic Church as it then existed.

After a while, and through the inevitable operation of architectural evolution - there is no need to narrate the story of all the changes in this connection - the superintendency and direction of building operations (I am still referring to church and cathedral and similar structures) passed gradually into the hands of laymen. Of these great lay architects, especially those who worked in France where Gothic reached its utmost pinnacle of glory, we have many memorials and remains; in a large number of cases we have rather complete biographical sketches and even portraits. From all these records we know that the builders of this particular period were also loyal sons of the Mother Church.

It was so in England as well as in France, for we find in the Old Charges that the mason, when he came to unite with the Fraternity, was required to swear to be faithful and true to the Holy Church as well as to the King. But after the Reformation had established itself in England - which was quite a while after the death of Henry VIII - these operative masons, along with the rank and file of men in all other walks of life, became Protestants, - that is, they became members of the Church of England.

When does the story of Operative Masons begin? Give the dates of the "Middle Ages." What was the outstanding feature, or characteristic, of Romanesque architecture? Of Gothic? Who were the first architects of Gothic? What, do you suppose, led the bishops to take such an interest in building? To what church did masons then belong? Did they all have to belong to that church? If so, why? Why did laymen come to take the place of bishops as architects, or masters of the work? Where, do you suppose, may one find the records of these old-time master builders? Where did Gothic architecture reach its highest development? What religion was enjoined by the Old Charges? What is meant by "Old Charges"? What was the Reformation? When did it occur? What did Luther have to do with it? Henry VIII? What was the difference between a Protestant church, as we now know it, and the "Church of England"? What effect did Protestantism have on the religion of masons ?

In many histories of Freemasonry the account of the religious beginnings of the Craft stops off short at this place, but that is an error, a very misleading error, and one that should be carefully avoided by the Masonic student. Freemasonry as it became organized in 1717, and as we now know it, owed much, very much, to the operative builders of the Middle Ages, but it also owed, much, perhaps quite as much, to other sources, which had nothing whatever to do with operative building. I refer to esoteric societies and associations, and to scattered sources out of which many streams of influence gradually made their way into the main currents of Speculative Freemasonry.

In the time of Pope Innocent III (approximately in the year 1200) there began the great Albigensian Crusades. The purpose of this immense military advance into southern France was to stamp out flourishing communities of men and women who had come to believe in a Christianity very different from that represented by the pope. These men have been described as "Protestants before the Reformation." In a strict sense they were not Protestant, and their ideas were very far away from those made familiar to us by our own great Protestant denominations, but these men cherished independence of mind, purity of conduct, and demanded for themselves liberty of worship. They were the "heretics." I am myself convinced - though there is not here room to furnish the data on which my conviction rests - that these "heretics" set loose in Europe a powerful stream of influence, some of which finally found its way into Freemasonry. (See "New Light on the Renaissance," by Harold Bayley, among scores of other books.)

All our historians, at least nearly all of them, agree that Freemasonry owes very much to certain occult societies or groups that flourished - often in secret - during the late Middle Ages, and even into the after-Reformation times. Chief among these were the Rosicrucians and the Knights Templar. The Knights Templar had been in the East; they had come into contact with Jewish, Greek, and Arabic lore, and they had imbibed strange new ideas from far-away types of Christianity. The authorities of the Roman Catholic Church attacked these knightly orders on the ground that they had become heretics - "Gnostics" was the exact word used. Those who have most carefully examined the evidence (some Henry Charles Lea's great works on the period) are inclined to believe that the charges were more or less well grounded. The Knights Templar had become infected with heresy.

As for the Rosicrucians, not much is known about them and it is doubtful if much ever will be known about them, but it is certain that during the seventeenth century there were many powerful and original thinkers in Europe, especially in Germany, the Low Countries, and in England, who called themselves "Rosicrucians" and who made wide use of a (now) strange system of symbols and esoteric means of communication. It is believed by some that Francis Bacon was a Rosicrucian. I said that not much is known with certainty about them; of this one thing, however, we can be certain: they were Protestants, when they were not altogether outside the bounds of Christianity.

About the Kabbalists more is known. The literature called the Kabbala came into existence in Spain during the thirteenth century, or thereabouts, and won its way among the Jews who had grown weary of the sterile rationalism of Maimonides and his school. The Kabbalistical literature was dramatically brought to the attention of the intellectual circles of Europe by Reuchlin when, in or about 1500, he caught it up as a means of preventing a terrible slaughter of Jews by the papists. The Kabbala is a work of Jewish mysticism. From it there came into Freemasonry, so there is good reason to believe, the Legend of the Lost Word, the Tradition of Solomon's Temple, the Tradition of the Substitute Word, the Great Pillars, etc.

Can you name three Masonic histories? Which one is supposed to be the best? What is meant by "esoteric"? Can you tell anything about Pope Innocent III? What is meant by the word "heretic"? Can you tell anything about the Albigensian Crusades? Do you believe that Freemasonry connects in any way with the Knights Templar? Are the Masonic Knights Templar identical with the Order spoken of above? Why was the Order suppressed? Who was the last Grand Master of the Knights? Have you ever heard of Jacques de Molay? What can you tell about the Rosicrucians? Where were the Rosicrucians strongest? Describe the Kabbalists? Where did Kabbalism originate? When did Reuchlin live? What did he do? What does Freemasonry owe to Kabbalism? Was the Kabbala Jewish or Christian? If Freemasonry descended from the Kabbalists, and the other sources named above, as well as from Operative Masons of the Middle Ages, what, would you say, was the first religion of Freemasonry?

It should be further noted that during the century immediately preceding the famous Revival (1717) many men came into the Fraternity who where - to a certain extent - what would now be called Free Thinkers. This is not to say that they were atheists or anti-religious; it means that they chose to think for themselves, and were not able to accept many things officially taught by the churches. Quite a number of the founders and early champions of the Royal Society (this fact is overlooked so often) were active Freemasons, and so were many other learned men in different quarters who, in that period of rationalism, did not adhere to any religion at all, albeit, like Voltaire and the Deists, they believed in a Supreme Being. It is certain that many of these men found their way into the Fraternity at a period before the Revival and I have no doubt that they had something to do at the time with the complete releasing of Freemasonry from adhesion to any one religion whatsoever. The great paragraph "Concerning God and Religion" which Anderson (or whoever it was) incorporated in the first Grand Lodge Constitutions, is a frank statement to the effect that whereas in ancient times Freemasons had been obliged to be of the religion of the country in which they lived, that now no religious demands would be made of them save that they were not to be "stupid atheists" or "irreligious libertines". The adoption of the paragraph marks an epoch in the evolution of religion in the English-speaking world. It was a great magna charta of spiritual liberty proclaimed at a time when religious bigotry was more bigoted than ever, and when men were suffering all manner of persecution for daring to disagree with the official dogmas of the churches. The Masonic student should make the most careful study of this period of Masonic history because it was at this time that the constitutions and landmarks were adopted (many of them, anyhow) that are still in force, and it is to that period that Grand Lodges almost always turn when seeking for precedents whereon to establish new laws or regulations or interpretations. Unless one clearly grasps the principles built into Speculative Freemasonry at that time, he will ever remain hopelessly in the dark about the underlying principles of Freemasonry as it now exists.

What is meant by a Free Thinker? Is he anti-religious? Who are some typical Free Thinkers now? What was the Royal Society? When and by whom was it founded? Who were the Deists? What did they believe? What was the substance of the famous paragraph "Concerning God and Religion"? Who wrote the Constitutions? Who was Anderson? In what sense was that aforementioned paragraph a great religious magna charta? Why do Grand Lodges seek precedents in the period of the Revival? When and what was this Revival?

As time went on it came to pass that Freemasonry began to grow at a great rate, and it was inevitable, owing to the serious and religious character of the ritual, that many of the men drawn to it should be churchmen, or otherwise devout. A trend toward Christianization of the Order set in. In 1760 the Holy Bible was made a Great Light. In 1813, at the time of the famous Union of the two Grand Lodges, the Antient and the Modern, Freemasonry was specifically declared to be consecrated to the glory of God. After this the tide toward

Christianization set in with new power until it at last culminated in the work of Dr. George Oliver, whose name should be held in everlasting remembrance among Masons. To Oliver the whole Masonic system was essentially biblical and wholly Christian. He was so fruitful in influence, his books were so many, and his followers so numberless, that for decades men entirely lost sight of the original principles of Speculative Masonry - that Masonry, I mean, that is usually referred back for its origin to 1717. Indeed, that impulse has not yet by any means spent itself; many brethren, misled by the predominantly Scriptural cast of the Work, and misunderstanding a few scattered references here and there, assume that in some sense Freemasonry is specifically a Christian institution, and forget, the while, the presence of a great number of Jews in the Order, not to mention many who adhere to no one religion whatsoever. So late as 1887 Brother H.J. Whymper published a book since become standard, "The Religion of Freemasonry," in which he boldly upheld the thesis that Freemasonry is a specifically Christian institution. The work was introduced by W.J. Hughan, and edited by G. W. Speth.

It is probable that Brother Whymper (I join with all in honoring a name so illustrious in our annals) forgot the great and epoch-making Proclamation issued by H.R.H. the Duke of Sussex, M.W. Grand Master of the United Grand Lodge of England, published from Kensington Palace, July 2, 1842, which Proclamation plainly declared that Freemasonry is not the property of any one religion, and that those subjects of the Crown in India who were otherwise eligible and who could make a sincere profession of faith in one living God, be they Hindus or Mohammedans, might petition for membership in Freemasonry. That Proclamation established a precedent of vast influence, so that today the Fraternity flourishes in the Far East to an undreamed of extent, and it is quite impossible, in view of the fact of Masonic universality, to claim for any one religion, as against all others, the adhesion of this Order.

When was the Holy Bible made a great Light? Why is it called The Volume of the Sacred Law? Are there other Volumes of the Sacred Law? What book is so used by Jews? By Mohammedans? By Hindus? When was the lodge formally declared consecrated to God? Why do Masons speak of Him as T.S.G.A.O.T.U.? What was the

"Antient" Grand Lodge? The "Modern"? What is the Grand Lodge of England now called? What position did Dr. Oliver take? Do you agree with him? What book did Whymper publish? When? What was his position? When did H.R.H. the Duke of Sussex publish his Proclamation? And where? What was the significance of it? What does that proclamation mean for us? Does the Grand Lodge of England recognize lodges that accept men other than Christian?

The Bible is the sacred book of Christians; the ritual of Freemasonry is steeped in the Bible: therefore Freemasonry must be considered a Christian institution; this is the logic, expressed or implied, by which men have been led to hold that the Craft adheres to that one religion as against all others. These brethren should be made to understand the facts in the case. It is true that the Holy Bible was the ultimate source of much in the ritual but one needs only try to test the ritual by biblical references to find that after all the ritual is not built on the text of the Bible, for the great major incidents in the ritual - and this applies to all the grades - are not found in the Book at all. To cite but one example; the tragedy of Hiram Abiff which is so central to all the mysteries of Masonry, is not met with in any of the sacred books. The explanation of this lies ready to hand. Traditions and legends, suggested long ago by incidents in the Bible, were taken up here and there by different groups and worked over into new shapes and to new purposes. A luxuriant undergrowth of legend and myth sprang up about the feet of the old Bible stories, of which fact the rich old tales of Arthur and his Table and of the Search for the Grail, woven by Tennyson into the deeply colored and mystical poems of *The Idylls of the King*, may serve as a familiar example. Medieval religion, art, and architecture, as everybody knows, are all steeped in these old traditions, many of which had undergone an evolution that led them to become completely cut away from their original sources in the Sacred Writings.

The biblical traditions in Freemasonry did not come into it directly from the Bible, but from these other and secondary sources, and in long round-about paths, so that, by the time they had come to be incorporated into the ritual, they had undergone many profound transformations, so that it is no longer possible to call them biblical, save as such traditions as the above mentioned Holy Grail may also be called biblical. The Legend of the Lost Word, of the Substitute Word, of the great Temple of which Hiram Abiff was Grand Master, etc., etc., all had, no doubt, their first inspiration in the biblical narratives, but they have since traveled so far away from their sources that they may be thought of, like the old myths of the Greeks, as belonging to the whole world, and to men of all religions.

But while it is true that Freemasonry cannot be claimed by any one religion - no intelligent Freemason will make such a claim, however devout he may be in his own faith - it has a religious foundation that is all its own. Believing that there is under all the creeds one universal religion, which may be described as a belief in one God as the Father of all, in the immortality of the soul, and in the brotherhood of man, it demands of all its initiates adhesion to these root truths. What other things they may choose to believe, and how they may interpret or elaborate these fundamentals, is left wholly to their own private judgment. It is as if the Fraternity said to its children, "Here is the great substructure, the mother rock under your feet, on which you must each one build your own house of religion; what manner of temples you build, and in what style, and where, and how high, that I shall leave to you individually; but on the substructure of belief in God, in brotherhood, and in immortality, you must build, else you do not belong to me.

Give examples of biblical references in the Work. Recite portions of it that are drawn directly from the Bible. Have you ever sought for the origin of the Hiram Abiff tragedy in the Old Testament? What did you find? Does our account of Solomon's Temple agree with the account in the Book of Kings? How have you explained this to yourself ? What do you think of the explanations as given above? Have you ever read Tennyson's *Idylls of the King*? Who was Tennyson? When did he live? Can you give the story of the Holy Graal (sometimes spelled "Grail")? Retell in your own words the account of how traditions, originally from the Bible, reached us by circuitous paths, and after they had become worked over and changed. What is the "religion" of Freemasonry?

PART XIV
UNIVERSALITY

IN ALL the lore of Freemasonry nothing more appeals to the imagination of the young initiate than the story of how travelers have found Freemasons among the wilds, and how our mysteries have been discovered amid the most ancient peoples, in old China, in Central America, "in Egypt 40,000 years ago." These stories are as romantic as Kipling's bloody tale, *The Man Who Would be King*, which is itself a hint of the universal existence of the Craft, because they appeal to the imagination, and conjure up the picture of a Fraternity which has always existed, and now exists everywhere. One must be on his guard against these stories, for it is fatally easy to fabricate them; if a man sets out to prove a theory he usually can dig up something somewhere to serve as evidence, like those

> . . . "Learn'd philologists, who chase
> A panting syllable through time and space,
> Start it at home, and hunt it in the dark
> To Gaul, to Greece, and into Noah's Ark."

But even so, many of the accounts of the universal diffusion of Masonic secrets and traditions are as well authenticated as anything we have, and are not to be despised, though a man be ever so high-brow a critic. And though they are to have each and everyone a question mark placed after them, they nevertheless serve to give to one's mind a kind of composite picture of the Universality of Freemasonry, than which there is no nobler theme inside the pale of the Great Teachings which it is now our province to be studying.

I believe that it is safe to say that now, at this present moment, and as a matter of fact, Freemasonry is Universal, - and that for many reasons.

It may be that the body of Freemasonry, as we know it, came into existence a few hundred years ago; but the soul of Freemasonry, its spirit, many of its principles and its symbols, have been among men from a time since which the memory of man runneth not to the contrary. In China, in the ruins of ancient Latin-American civilizations (I have just seen the carving of a Masonic apron - so it is interpreted by the authorities - on a plaque taken from a city of the Mayas that is several thousand years old, how many thousands I can't recall), throughout medieval Europe, among the so-called Dark Ages, in Ancient Rome, Greece, Egypt, and even in India, one may here and there encounter organizations, teachings, emblems, and symbols that are singularly like our own. Some things in our Fraternity have evidently existed everywhere and always.

This diffusion through past times is only equaled by the cosmopolitanism of Masonry as it now is. If one travels in the far north, in Siberia or in Alaska, he may encounter a Masonic lodge. If he goes into the Sandwich Islands (as at Papeete) or to the last reaches of southern Australia, he may come upon a building bearing the square and compasses. There are lodges in China and Japan, in the Malay Archipelago, in India, in the Balkans, and in the midst of Africa. Masonry has its center everywhere: its circumference nowhere.

The evolution of the Craft reveals a steady progress from an institution that once was attached to one church and to one task to an institution that now over-reaches all the creeds as the sky over-arches the earth, and accepts the responsibility of a thousand tasks. In that history one encounters an event which stands as a high light in the history of the human spirit, - the utterance "Concerning God and Religion" in the Constitutions of 1723 - and which is the noblest expression of the spiritual universality of the Order that we know.

"A Mason is obliged by his tenure, to obey the moral law; and if he rightly understands the Art, he will never be a stupid Atheist or irreligious Libertine. But though in ancient times Masons were charged in every country to be of the religion of that country or nation, whatever it was, yet it is now thought more expedient only to oblige them to that religion in which all men agree, leaving their particular opinions to themselves: that is to be Good men and True, or men of Honor and Honesty, by whatever Denomination or Persuasion they may be distinguished; whereby Masonry becomes the Centre of Union and the Means of conciliating true Friendship among persons that must have remained at a perpetual distance."

Of this it has been well said that if "that statement had been written yesterday, it would be remarkable enough. But when we consider that it was set forth in 1723, amidst bitter sectarian rancor and intolerance unimaginable, it rises up as forever memorable in the history of men! The man who wrote that document, did we know his name, is entitled to be held till the end of time in the grateful and venerative memory of the human race. The temper of the times was all for relentless partisanship, both in religion and in politics." In that famous Article the prophetic soul of Masonry, "brooding over years to come," anticipated the highest triumphs of the genius of tolerance which was yet to be, so that Crawley could well say that "in the eyes of the philosophical historian, the proudest boast of our society must always be, that in the Revival of our Craft A. D. 1717, we distinctively adopted the doctrines which found expression two generations later, in the Philanthropy of Howard and the humanity of a Wilberforee."

Of a piece with this famous pronouncement was the Act of Union in 1813. During the long process through which the Fraternity was achieving its unity out of the particularism of the old days of transition it was inevitable that there should be misunderstandings, schisms, feuds, and jealousies: all these came to a head in 1750 or thereabouts in the open warfare between the rival Grand Lodges, the so-called "Modern" and the so-called "Ancient." For long it appeared that the Order, like the religious, political, and social institutions of the time, was merely talking about a unity and a universality that it had neither the will nor the power to bring into existence: but at last Freemasonry overcame its own internal feud, which had been as bitter as the rivalry between two churches, and thus demonstrated that men can do such things, if they but have the mind.

These two outstanding events, the Act of Union, and the adopting of the great paragraph concerning God and Religion, remain unto this day to inspire every Mason to believe that union is possible among men, however diverse they may be in interest and creed: more, they cheer and encourage because they demonstrate that it can be accomplished, and such a demonstration is worth more than many homilies. So long as we have those two outstanding triumphs to look back to we need never lose hope for the ultimate unity of the whole Masonic world, and the whole non-Masonic world. Union and universality, such things axe not mere visions, dreamed by poets in solitary cells.

Give as many examples as you can to show the antiquity of Masonry. Do you believe that Freemasonry has everywhere and always existed? Who were the Mayas? Did the ancient Chinese have Freemasonry? Do the American Indians? Is it the same as ours, if so? How do you account for it? We have Masonic documents written more than 500 years ago: how widespread was Freemasonry then? Where and in what shape did it exist in the ancient world? In what countries now existing would you fail to find Freemasonry?

Furthermore, the Fraternity as it now exists, with all its faults upon it, is, as I like to think, itself the great argument for the coming of unity among men. For consider. Men of all races, of all colors, of almost every creed, tongue, nation, and location are now, as an actual fact, Masons, and therefore bound to all the rest of us, however far away we may be in all those particulars, by a tie that is growing stronger every year. Not always does that tie hold - the Great War broke it - but it is a tie nevertheless, and there will come a time when no war will be able to snap it in twain. If each one of us could see the world as God is able to see it, not at one point, and for a moment, and then in a most faulty fashion, but as a whole, calmly, clearly, understandingly, I am sure that we should see the Masonic Fraternity standing there among men as one of the noblest of all the noble things in that vision; like the moon breaking through the clouds on a stormy night would be its tender brotherhood and its constant yearning and striving for more brotherhood; and its refusal to be defeated or balked when brotherhood, for a time, fails or is broken.

We need not hesitate to acknowledge the many defeats which the ideal of Universality has suffered even in the house of its friends but every such fact, if we are to be true to things as they really are, must be confronted by this further fact, - That Universality in Masonry, for all its failures, is a living and therefore a shaping ideal. One wishes that he might write those last words in some new way to make them dig deep into a reader's mind in order to avoid the pitfall of a too easy thinking of them. An ideal is a force to be reckoned with, and not a dream hanging helpless in the void. Masons believe in Universality; they strive for it; they shape things to bring it about; they make sacrifices in its behalf; they are always, in proportion as they truly understand their art, eager to let differences lie if so be that they can bring men closer to men. That being true there is no need ever to feel discouragement because the perfect day has not yet come; if we were all doing mere lip service to our ideal, pessimism might be justifiable, but not as long as we strive for universal brotherhood.

Moreover, it is wise for us, even when confronted by some apparent failure of Universality, to see that failure as it actually is, and not as it is hurriedly reported to be. There is in point, for example, the long disagreement between the Grand Orient of France and the Grand Lodge of England, and other Grand Lodges in the world. That break in Masonic fellowship is made use of by our enemies more than any other thing to heap sarcasm upon Masonic aspirations towards unity. Well, that rupture is an unfortunate thing for all sides, view it how we may, but just what does it amount to? It amounts to this, that the Masons living under these two Grand Lodge systems cannot visit in each other's lodges, or approve one or two of each other's doctrines. But there is no enmity. Masons under the Grand Orient do not make war on English Masons. They do not hate each other. In all ways now possible they aid and assist each other. In all ways, save in those ways controlled by the lack of formal recognition, French Masons and other Masons live in amity and brotherhood. Some day the breach will be healed.

In carrying out their ideal there is no reason why Masons may not make free use of all the agencies now employed generally to further internationalism, understanding among peoples, and mutual intercourse. The scientists have their congresses, business men have their conventions, statesmen their conferences: one may hope to see American Grand Lodges use these same instrumentalities in behalf of a better understanding among nations. The Trowel is the working tool of the Master Mason; we must make use of it now more than ever, while a discordant and broken world lies about us. It is unfortunate that certain of our leaders hesitate to use the Trowel lest they mar its shining surface, forgetting the while that it is to be used and not looked at.

In what way does the evolution of Masonry prove it to be universal in character? Can you describe the early part of the eighteenth century in England? Whom do you believe to have been responsible for the Article concerning God and Religion? Can you give an example of the bitter partisanship of those times in religion? What was the religious character of Operative Masonry? Why did it cut itself loose from any one religion? How did the "Ancient" Grand Lodge originate? Describe its feud with the "Modern." How was the Union brought about? If those two bodies were able to unite, could not churches unite? Do you believe that our Grand Lodges should resume fraternal relations with German Masonry? Does the tie now hold between English and Irish Masonry? Does the fact that Masonry can unite all prove anything as regards political relations, churches, etc.? If so, what?

What is an ideal? What is the relation between ideal and fact? Is a true ideal a "fact on the way"? In what way does Universality remain an ideal? Are you in favor of recognizing the Grand Orient? If not, why not? Do you hate French Masons because you do not agree with them? How can Masonry use the Trowel? What agencies are at hand which we might use to bring about better international relations? Should Masonry assist to bring about better political relations between countries? How and why?

The necessary implications of Universality, so it seems to me, are not enough understood. Universality being a fact and a living ideal, certain things follow, and these it is well to consider.

It is evident that an Order which speaks a message to a world has found something that the world can understand and needs. Its acts, its principles, and its symbols are a kind of great Esperanto which perpetually translates itself into the languages of all men everywhere. Diverse as are the conditions under which men live, political, social, economic, and religious, men have certain common needs. Just as it has ever been one of the great desiderata of statecraft to discover a common ground whereon nations might meet politically, so has it ever been one of the great hopes of men to find such a ground in morality, and in the human things of life. It is evident that Freemasonry has made that discovery. What it has to give is what men everywhere feel the need of, else it would remain, as almost all institutions do, a merely local and transitory thing. The things that Freemasonry have to give are simple enough, and to us may be commonplace, but just as it required a great social genius to discover an alphabet, which children can learn and all men can use, so has it necessitated an equal genius to discover just those things, and their right combination, to meet the needs of men everywhere. The fact that Masonry is everywhere welcomed as soon as it is discovered and its nature understood, gives us each one a heightened confidence in that which Masonry is.

Also, the Universality of Masonry implies that human nature is everywhere the same, which fact, though it may be familiar enough to most of us, is not by any means admitted by many of a different faith. Socrates counted it a great day when he discovered that behind the varying languages and dialects and nodes of thought and expression all men had the same kind of mind: Spencer found himself in a new world of thought when he at last saw that "humanity is an organism." "Men change," said the wise Goethe, "but man remains the same." Racial distinctions, sex, color, language, creeds, governments, these have broken our human family into diverse and often quarrelling groups: but while men change in language, in theories and in customs from generation to generation, there is that in man which does not change, either in time or place, a common humanity which ever remains the same, and stretches under the world, as the earth retains her unbroken identity beneath the many inequalities of her surface. From the mist-hung distance of the remotest times down unto our own hour man has thought, loved, labored, dreamed, prayed, hated, fought the while he has walked "the dim and perilous way of life." His spirit has sought goodness, truth, and beauty, and he has evermore craved the companionship of his fellows. It is the misfortune of too many creeds, moralities and sects, be they political, social, or religious, that they cater to the accidental and temporary needs of men, and too often divide rather than unite our hard-driven struggling race. It is the glory of Freemasonry that it speaks the revealing word to that in each of us which is universal, thereby helping to build in the midst of the years "an institution of the dear love of comrades" in which the mind is free to think, the hand to do, and the heart to love. William Penn believed that death would remove our masks and that we would all then discover ourselves to be of one religion. The Universality of Freemasonry lifts the masks of all differences and proves that we are now all united in our humanity, that God has made of one blood all nations that dwell upon the face of the earth.

In regards to morality and religion this seems especially true. There is much in the morality of every people that cannot help being local and therefore temporary; and this is not to be held against it because a morality, if it function at all, must adjust itself to the details of life; but if an institution tie itself too rigidly to those local things in morality it cannot possibly function among another people, where conditions are so different. Some men believe that all morality is purely local, made up of prejudices and accidents, and that there is no ethic everywhere valid. Masonry contradicts this. Masonry proves itself wiser than many other institutions, because it, in the words of Albert Pike, "is the universal morality, suitable to the inhabitants of every clime, to the man of every creed."

Freemasonry makes no attempts to adjudicate the religious quarrels of man. It does not take the position that there is one true religion among a great many religions wholly false, nor does it take the opposite position that all religions are equally indifferent. Its position is entirely its own. It takes the position that, letting religions be as they are, they one and all possess certain fundamentals everywhere alike, and it is on these fundamentals that Masonry takes its stand. In a letter which a Deputy District Grand Master once wrote to George William Speth there occurred this sentence:

"I have just initiated Moung Ban Ahm, a Burman, who has so far modified his religious beliefs as to acknowledge the existence of a personal God. The Worshipful Master was a Parsi, one Warden a Hindu, or Brahmin, the other an English Christian, and the Deacon a Mohammedan" Mr. Ahm believed in the existence of God, in the immortality of the soul, and in the brotherhood of man: that was sufficient. He was not disturbed in whatever other beliefs he had because if a man holds to the three mentioned his religion can function inside the Masonic Fraternity. And once in the Fraternity he could find no reason to quarrel with his brother the Brahmin, or his other brother the Christian, or his brother the Mohammedan, because in every case the doctrines peculiar to each were not called for in Masonic workings, and therefore such doctrines could have no chance to come into conflict. Inasmuch as the only religious doctrines that operate in Masonry are belief in a personal God, in immortality, and in brotherhood, the man who holds them is, for Masonry, sufficiently equipped, and Masonry has no reason to find fault with whatever he may further believe: and because nearly all men in the world, be they ever so far removed from us in America, believe in those three great doctrines, and because Masonry builds upon them, Masonry may be said to have a genuine religious Universality. And this, if you will consider a moment, is a very great thing: because prophets and leaders and teachers and religions without number have ever been searching for just such a foundation.

But even if early Masons had hit upon so universal a foundation for a Fraternity it would have availed little had they not at the same time devised a form of organization equally universal. It is worth while to consider this a moment, because it is almost never discussed. History furnishes us with an illustration whereby it can be quickly considered for our present purposes. Why was it that the Reformation, as launched by Luther, soon grew stagnant, and became a merely local German affair? It was because in Germany it was suffered to flow into the mould of German social life, and this mould not existing elsewhere, the Reformation was unable to function outside Germany. The spirit and doctrines of the Reformation were there but Luther and his followers were notable to give them a vehicle wherein to travel into other countries. Now it was the peculiar glory of Calvin that he was able to give the Reformation just such an organization as enabled him and his followers to take it anywhere. They devised for it a vehicle that would serve as well in France as in Germany, and in Scotland as in France, and it was therefore owing to Calvin that the Reformation became, so far as the Western world is concerned, a universal thing. Early Freemasonry might have been as true in principle and spirit as it now is and yet, for lack of vehicular means, have remained a local English sect, or club. Fortunately it was not so, and that because our forbears possessed a genius for organization equal to that for thinking.

Freemasonry is not the only great institution in society, nor is it responsible for healing over all the divisions of the world, be they religious, political, social, economic, racial, or what not: but it has found a way to surmount those barriers in order to penetrate into every land, and that is sufficient for its purpose. Because of this it has an unlimited future.

"There are works yet left for Freemasonry to accomplish greater than the twelve labors of Hercules." Many of these labors lie inside the Craft itself where there still remain many obstacles to internal Unity, and therefore to external Universality. There are many Masonic rites in the field and these are not always working together as smoothly as they should. There are Masonic bodies of the same rite that do not always agree, as is the case now among a few of the Grand Lodges of Mexico. And, as already mentioned, the sundering of peoples by the late War has broken the unity of the Order. It is a part of our task to heal over these divisions. It is a part of our task to make Masonic unity prevail.

What does Masonry have to give that all men need? Do other institutions have it to give? In what sense is it true that men are everywhere the same? Do you agree with Spencer that "humanity is an organism"? What is Masonic morality? Why is it more universal in character than other moralities? Why is it that the Masonic organization can everywhere function? Can you think of other organizations of which this is true?

PART XV
THE FATHERHOOD OF GOD

MANY attempts have been made to expound Freemasonry's teaching concerning God by recourse to the peculiar phraseology that is employed in the ritual, but these attempts have always broken down because the ritualistic language has been fashioned, not for the purposes of exact theological thinking, but for symbolical and ritualistic purposes. God is not in fact an architect; such a term is very misleading. It suggests a great artificer who made the worlds out of nothing, or else out of crude material, and who went about it as a carpenter might frame a house. Such a Being would necessarily exist apart from the thing He has made, as a machinist is apart from the mechanism he contrives. The modern mind will have nothing to do with such ideas because men have learned that God cannot be conceived of as living and working apart from the universe, but must somehow be involved in that universe. The Masonic thinker can escape from these difficulties by remembering that in the ritual God is described as T.G.A.O.T.U., not because such words describe His nature as Masonry understands it, but because such an appellation is in harmony with the architectural language of the ceremonies.

Freemasonry, nowhere offers a definition of the nature and attributes of God, but leaves such matters to each individual to fashion as best he can. It asks of a man only that he believe that God is. It does not even try to prove the existence of God, after the fashion of the dogmatic theologians, but assumes that its candidates already have that belief in their hearts.

However, it appears that while Freemasonry does not define its conception of God certain attributes are assumed by the Masonic system as a whole, and taken for granted throughout it, so that while these attributes are nowhere insisted upon explicitly, they are a necessary postulate of Masonic teachings as a whole. I may be wrong in this; if I am, it will not greatly matter, because this paper, like the others in this series, is designed to be not exhaustive but suggestive, and prepared as a paper for discussion, rather than as an official treatise.

What is the "peculiar phraseology" referred to? Have you considered that such a name truly describes God? Did you gain any conception of God while taking the work? What are the objections to the theory that God exists apart from the universe? In what way can God be involved in the universe? What is the nature of the theological language employed in the ritual? Does Freemasonry anywhere define or describe the attributes of God? What is meant by "attributes"? How would you prove the existence of God? What is an atheist? What is meant by the phrase "necessary postulate"?

In its most fundamental sense - the only sense in which Freemasonry teaches it - the Fatherhood of God means that when a human being comes into existence there is somewhat in him (let us not try to define it) that derives immediately from God's own being; and that through all his existence - which we believe to be endless - this man's being remains rooted in God's own being, so that if God Himself were to cease to be he would also, and at the same instant, cease to be. In the language of metaphysics the relation between God and man is ontological. It exists in the nature of things, so that neither God nor man could cause it not to be; and it does not depend upon a man's religious beliefs, or upon any other belief or opinion. All men, whatever be their faith or fortune, from Plato down to the African dwarf, have this relation with God. What God is to any one He is to every other one, and all that God can be to or do for any man, He is to and does for all men equally, and everlastingly. This eternal and universal Fatherhood in Him does not come into existence when we begin to believe it; it is already a fact before we believe it, and remains a fact whether we believe it or not.

The Fatherhood of God is more than a symbol it is a fact, albeit of a very different nature from human fatherhood. By God's love is meant that our being is rooted in Him, and that He is ever doing for us all that a God can do. His relation to us is neither purchased nor given but holds in the very structure of life itself. It does not rest on sentiment or emotion but in the nature of things, so that it is a great blunder to suppose that because God is our Father therefore He can, at will, reverse the processes of the universe or set aside the everlasting laws of things. He remains our Father through all our experiences, but not for that reason are we shielded from pain, from loss, and from the extreme horrors into which our own or the world's ignorance, or the vicissitudes of fortune may bring us. Nevertheless, whatever be our lot, it is the great secret of our courage to know that the show and scheme of things is not swirling about us in the wind of chance, but that our lives are rooted in One who thoroughly understands us; and that, whatever betide the inner stuff of our nature cannot dissolve away into dust, or our beings be brought to extinction. Our belief in God's Fatherhood - so this is to say - does not create the fact, but it makes the fact a power in our conscious thought, and that is a mighty thing.

"The doctrine of Fatherhood in God is a doctrine of faith. It is a belief about the interior mystery of the Infinite supported by much, and opposed by much, in the experience of mankind. It is a belief about the universe, in behalf of our human world, supported by all that is best in that world; it is fitted to elevate, energize, gladden and console human beings; it is the belief that generates and justifies all other high beliefs. If God is the Absolute goodness and compassion, our human world is His concern, all righteousness has His approval, all efforts at righteousness are followed by His sympathy, all sin must reckon with His endless enmity, all penitence may count upon His pity, all strivings at reform may be sure of His inspiration, all union in the endeavor to cleanse the earth of moral evil may move in the tides of His Spirit, all grief may find consolation in His infinite love, all loss may hope to become, in the courses of the ages, eternal gain in Him. If Fatherhood in God is the ultimate reality in the Infinite, as the Infinite is related to our human world, that world is glorious with meaning and with hope."

What is your own conception of the Fatherhood of God? How do we know that God exists? How do we know that He is a Father in the sense described? How is his Fatherhood to be reconciled with the evil and the suffering of the world? What does belief in God's Fatherhood do for a man? Is such a belief required of a Mason? In what way does Freemasonry teach the Fatherhood of God? What is taught concerning this subject in the Old and the New Testaments?

The Fatherhood of God is not anywhere explicitly taught by Freemasonry but it is everywhere implied, so that the great doctrines peculiar to the Craft demand it for their guarantor, and make inevitably toward it The Brotherhood of Man could never come to pass if the peoples of the world were by their very nature different from each other; it would be as impossible to bridge over such chasms as it is now impossible to bring our race into an equal brotherhood with beasts or trees.

So also is it with Equality. It is impossible for us ever to be, as I have already tried to show in this series, of the same fortune or ability, because the conditions in which we necessarily live make for endless variety, and that is of itself a kind of inequality: but there is a region beneath all such differences in which we find ourselves at one. God is to the most ignorant wretch all that a God can be, and does all things possible for him, so that in such matters that wretch is the equal of prophets and kings.

Our hope of Democracy is linked up with the Fatherhood of God. "Always, a new idea of man implies and involves a new conception of God. It was natural for the men who bowed low when the glittering chariot of Caesar swept along the streets of Rome to think of God as an omnipotent Emperor, ruling the world with an arbitrary and irresponsible almightiness. For men who live in this land of the free such a conception of God is a caricature. The citizens of a republic do not believe that God is an infinite autocrat, nor do they bow down to divine despotism; they worship in the presence of an Eternal Father, who is always and everywhere accessible to the humblest man who lifts his heart in prayer. Republican principles necessarily involve faith in the Fatherhood of God. The logic of the American idea leads to faith in a Divine Love universal and impartial, all encompassing and everlasting."

What is meant by saying that the doctrine of the Fatherhood of God is everywhere implied in Freemasonry? In what way does the

Brotherhood of Man depend on the Fatherhood of God? What is taught in the V.S.L. concerning the Brotherhood of Man? What is meant by Equality? In what way does God's Fatherhood make all men equal? What does the Declaration of Independence teach concerning Equality? What does the V.S.L. have to say about Equality? What is meant by Democracy? How is the Doctrine of Democracy related to the Doctrine of the Fatherhood of God? Could Democracy exist among a people who worship a despotic God?

PART XVI
ENDLESS LIFE

"Tis true; 'tis certain; man though dead retains Part of himself; the immortal mind remains."

THESE WORDS, written by Homer 3,000 years ago, remind us how that ages before the ferment of modem thought and all the crusades of our modern religions, men believed in immortality as we do now. If one were to push himself behind Homer into an age long anterior to his, and as ancient to him as his is to us, one would and men cherishing the same hope. Imhotep, the father of architecture in stone, builder to the Egyptian King Zoser, lived 5,000 years ago, but for all that he believed in immortality as did Homer. And so with those to whom Imhotep looked back as to those grown ancient to him; and also with them in their turn; and so on to the beginning of things when the first half-wild hunter paused long enough in his search of meat to gaze wistfully across lovely valleys, where floating gossamers reminded him how frail and how fleeting is human life.

It is useless to try to prove by logic or by demonstration the immortality of man. We believe it, there is an end of it! And we do not believe it because we have proved it, but we try to prove it because we already believe it. It is a hope, a kind of inward certainty which finds its support not in this fact or in that, but in the cast and color of life as a whole. It rises up into our minds like an exaltation from all our thoughts, all our experiences, all our dreams, as the odor that drifts across a summer field distills from numberless unnoted plants. We are never so puzzled as when we are challenged to give a reasoned proof of this hope: and we are never so unreasonable as when we cease to believe it. Men everywhere and always have believed it not because priests have taught them or because scientists have found out the secret of it, but because life itself has taught them, and it is something that the universe itself is always whispering to them. The priests and the churches have not created the belief: it is the belief that has made the priests and churches, and no amount of ignorance, baseness, or superstition appears able to blot out that great hope. The cannibals cling to it, and we ourselves though we sleep in a gutter, hear it announced within that whispering gallery which we call the soul.

"Though inland far we be,
Our souls have sight of that immortal sea
Which brought us hither."

How long have men believed in immortality? Who was Homer? Imhotep? Why do you believe in immortality? How would you set about to prove it? How do we know that men have always believed it?

It is impossible to form any mental picture of the future life. No two religions describe it in the same way, and some of them, ancient Buddhism, for example, have refused to describe it at all. Our modern spiritists who follow in the train of Sir Oliver Lodge, Conan Doyle, Camile Flammarion and their school, believe themselves to have received authentic news from the Beyond but unfortunately they have never been able to agree as to the nature of things in that unknown realm. It appears that such descriptions as are given through the mediums, Ouija Boards and such other occult means of communication usually conform in a general way to the preconceptions of the spiritists themselves. The Eskimo spiritist is told that heaven is a beautiful place full of icebergs and polar bears; the American Indian learns that it is a happy hunting ground; the Chinese spiritist - spiritism has been developed in China to a degree of respectability and perfection never attained elsewhere - is informed that heaven is a gloried China organized strictly in accord with the principles of ancestor worship. All this would indicate that if bona fide communications ever do penetrate the veil the conditions are such as to preclude the transmission of accurate or definite information, so that spiritists themselves are in like case with the rest of us who find that eye hath not seen nor ear heard nor hath it entered into the mind of man to conceive what the future life is like.

Nevertheless it is difficult to cherish even the thinnest hope of a continued life without trying to fashion some sort of conception of it, because the mind cannot otherwise handle the idea at all. Because we hold immortality as a belief we are compelled to think it as a thought, and it is this psychological necessity, perhaps, that has led men in every country and in all ages to make for themselves some picture of heaven. One should not try to quarrel with this, because one cannot do so successfully: man is so made that he must behave in this manner, and that is an end of it.

But it is for this reason, I believe, that we should be all the more careful that our thinking about the future life be strictly reasonable. If our nature compels us to think out some conception of immortality, that same nature similarly compels us to fashion a conception that won't insult the intelligence or fly in the face of known facts. It is necessary to be reasonable while we reason about Eternal Life. It seems to me - and I speak here only for myself - that this principle in itself is one of the teachings of Freemasonry concerning this subject. Our Fraternity leaves it to each individual to fashion his own conceptions of the Beyond but at the same time, and by all the arts at its command, persuades its votaries ever to remain in the Light, to seek more Light, and to fear to walk farther than the Light can lead them: and this Light itself is, of course, nothing other than reason, and knowledge, and right thinking. When the subject passes beyond into the darkness of the unknowable it is better to cease pursuing it further, lest we fall into superstition.

How do you picture the future life in your own mind? What is spiritism? Name a few leading spiritists now living. Do spiritists agree among themselves as to the future life? Give an example of some conception of the future life that is contradicted by facts as we know them, and that is unreasonable. Why should we try to make our picture of the future life as reasonable as possible?

It is both safe and wise to hold fast to the principle that all reality is bound up together into a great unity - for the which reason we call it a Universe - and that one part of this system does not contradict or give the lie to any other part. There is no good reason to suppose that death makes any profound change in the scheme of things. Death is a part of the Universe and always has been and, it may possibly prove, always will be. It is reasonable to suppose that the Universe will be the same after we are dead as it was before, and that therefore the "future life," as we call it (it is no longer "future" to those now living it) will in all essentials be of a piece with this present life. Why should we expect marvels, wonders, and impossibilities there when such things are not found here? What right have we to suppose that the experience of death will change our world out of all recognition, and transform ourselves into beings utterly different from what we are?

"What is human is immortal," said Bulwer-Lytton. Why is not the reverse also true? "What is immortal is human." We are here in closest relation to an earth, out of the surface of which we labor to wrest our bread each and every one of us is the member of one race - the human - and of some one grand division thereof, in consequence of which we differ greatly in color, language, appearance, and a hundred other things. The race as a whole is equally divided between two sexes, the members of which are so unlike each other in many important respects as to cause one to believe that sexual differences extend into the inmost recesses of human nature, and are not to be put on or off by any possible change. We are each one organized in a physical body, and it is ceaselessly necessary for us to work, to strive, to endure, to eat and sleep, and to suffer. It may be that all these things will be carried over into whatever life, or lives, may be waiting for us beyond. They are neither superficial nor accidental and are so woven into the general scheme of things that it is difficult to understand how human life could know itself after death with all such things omitted.

In spite of one's self such a discussion leads into theology, the most irritating of all subjects, and the least appropriate to these pages. In a field where no landmarks are marked out for us we are necessarily forced to fall back on private opinion, a thing I have done throughout this paper, and with the most cordial invitation to the reader to disagree if he is so disposed. I have no interest as a Mason in theological beliefs concerning the future life save to secure for ourselves a principle that will guarantee for us the full protection of the present life and all its values. It may be said that what a man believes about the future is his own private affair and should be respected as such. This is very true as long as the man's beliefs about the life to come do not seriously interfere with the life that now is, a thing that often happens. If my beliefs cause me to be illiberal or harsh, or unkind, or if they are such as to destroy my happiness, then my beliefs become matters of concern to my fellows, and they have a right to challenge me thereon. It is true, as I remarked above, that Freemasonry leaves the fashioning of this religious belief to the individual, nevertheless the Fraternity's spirit and teachings are distinctly opposed to beliefs that lead a man into unbrotherly behavior or unmasonic conduct. What Masonry has to teach concerning immortality is necessarily of a piece with its other teachings. If democracy, equality, charity, brotherly love, truth, kindliness, and honorable labor are good things now they cannot cease to be good things in the life to come. If such things are of God in this life it is hardly possible that they will cease to be divine in the next life.

If a man were to ask me point-blank, "what, in so many words, does Freemasonry teach about the endless life?" I should be hard put to make a reply "Freemasonry does not teach anything about it after the manner of an old-fashioned church catechism, but all its rites and ceremonies, its spirit and its laws are filled with immortality as the sky is suffused with light. Immortality is the motif of the Masonic symphony.

There is one word to be said in addition. In the great drama of the Third Degree there are things done and said that give one a new and enlarged conception of everlasting life. The initiate has it brought home to him that if there are some things which abide for ever, so that they are undestroyed by all the deaths that are, it is possible to search out such things now, and to mould his life about them, and give them the place of control at the center of the heart, so that one can live the eternal life in the midst of time. This is not easily gained, as many a man has learned to his cost: there are ruffians at the gates, lions in the path, and often it will seem to one who seeks this Royal Secret that his days are become a succession of deaths.

> "He who flagged not in the earthly strife,
> From strength to strength advancing - only he
> His soul well-knit, and all his battles won,

Mounts, and that hardly, to eternal life."

What do we mean by saying that we live in a universe? What is your theory about the part death plays in the life of man? What are the things in human nature least liable to change after death? What is meant by theology? What kind of beliefs about the future life cause men to be harsh and unkind? What has Masonry to teach concerning immortality? What is the meaning of the drama of the Third Degree? In what way does the Third Degree teach eternal life?

PART XVII
BROTHERLY AID

IT IS ONE of the principal uses of history that it enables us better to understand the present. We are ourselves so intimately related to our world as it now is, and this world is so complicated, that often it is quite impossible for us to form a true conception of it. But after a few decades have passed, and our own period detaches itself and becomes a unity, so that it can be viewed as a whole and as a thing by itself, it becomes greatly simplified; multitudes of bewildering details drop away, and it stands forth in its essentials, so that the historian can grasp it in its true proportions and relations. In this wise it often happens that in a certain true sense no age is understood until it has taken its place in history. This fact itself in turn can be brought about to enable one to view his own period as if it were a thing past, for it often happens that we discover some earlier period to be so like our own that to learn to understand that past period is to enable one's self to understand one's own. All this, which seems so remote from the theme of this paper, is written to explain why I shall begin the study of Brotherly Aid by a rapid sketch of a condition that developed itself among the Roman people many centuries ago. That condition, I believe, was the same in essentials as the condition in which we now live, so that by viewing it as a whole we can the better understand the social world in which we find ourselves.

In the early days of the Republic Roman life was a very stable thing, and Roman customs were almost stationary. A man grew up in the house in which he was born; when he married he brought his wife to live with him under the paternal roof; and when he died he left his own sons abiding in the same place. Neighboring families were similarly stable, and all these groups, owing to this perpetual neighborliness and to intermarriage, became so inwoven with each other that in a community there would be not one stranger. A man's life took root in such a community like a tree and grew there permanently. The individual was not left to his own private resources: he was surrounded by others who were ever at hand to aid him in misfortune, nurse him in illness, and mourn him in death. He was strong with the strength of his family and of his neighborhood, and this no doubt accounts for the sturdy manhood and womanhood of the early Romans.

But there came a time when the long enduring stability of Roman life was broken up. By gradual degrees the Romans conquered adjoining territory. A great military system was organized. Whole nations were brought into the Roman system. Alien peoples flocked into Italy, and new religions established their headquarters in Rome. The Republic gave way to the Empire, and the Senate succumbed to the Emperor. Great cities arose; travel was made possible; and a feverish restlessness took the place of the old stability. The old calm neighborhood life was destroyed and in its place there grew up a fermenting life in town and city. A man no longer lived and died in the place of his birth, but moved about from community to community, so that men became human tumbleweeds evermore shifting about from place to place as the windy currents of chance might carry them. It came to pass that a man lived a stranger in his own neighborhood, so that he scarce knew the other persons living under the same roof. He was thrown back on his own unaided individual resources in misfortune and in death. In the unequal struggle he often became morally bankrupt and the constant strain undermined his health. It was for such causes that Rome ultimately fell.

In this situation men set out about the creating of a bond that would take the place of the lost neighborhood ties. They organized themselves into Collegia. These groups were formed of men engaged in the same trade and they usually, in the early days of their history, were principally devoted to securing for a man a becoming burial service, the lack of which so filled a Roman with dread. But in the course of time these organizations - we could justly call them lodges - assumed more and more functions until at last a man found in them charities, social life, business aid, religious influences, friendship, and such other features of general protection as caused him to call his own group "My Mother Collegium." To live a stranger in a city was no longer a thing to dread to a man who could find in such a fellowship the same friendship and support that his forefather had secured in the old-time neighborhood.

What are the principal uses of history? Why is it difficult for us to understand our own time? How does history help to learn the present by means of the past? Describe conditions under which the early Romans lived. In what way did this make for a healthy manhood? How did these conditions protect a man from physical and moral bankruptcy? What broke up the stability of ancient Roman life? What was Rome's "immigration problem"? Was it like ours? What cause led to the breakdown of Roman character? What were Collegia? How were they organized and what purposes did they serve? How does the history of Freemasonry help you to understand Freemasonry as it now is? Did you live in childhood under conditions similar to those described?

It would be easy to compare with the rise and development of the Collegia the rise and development of the Church in the Middle Ages, for the latter came into existence to serve similar purposes; but there is no need of this, because the idea has already been made sufficiently clear. So is it also clear, I trust, that we men of today are living under just such conditions as brought the Collegia into existence, which is the one point of this historical excursion. The great majority of us are living in towns and cities; and almost all of us are subject to the unsettling conditions that shuttle us about from place to place, and from condition to condition, so that life has lost its firmness and security. We live in streets where our next door neighbor is a stranger to us; or in an apartment house or tenement where with dwellers on the same floor we have no ties at all. Our industrial system is such that vast numbers of us are ever moving about from one job to another, which fact is true also even of the farmers, the majority of whom are tenants, and therefore migratory. In the midst of such conditions the individual is often thrown wholly upon his own resources which is such an unnatural thing that many break under it. The restlessness and the ache of modern life are undoubtedly due in large measure to these facts.

But it is here that the lodge comes in, for the lodge, from this present point of view, is nothing other than a substitute for the old-fashioned small community life wherein neighbor was so tied to neighbor that there was no need of associated charities, social centers, or employment bureaus. In a lodge a man need no longer be a stranger: he finds there other men who, like himself, are eager to establish friendships, engage in social intercourse, and pool the resources of all in behalf of the needs of each. The fraternal tie redeems a man from loneliness and from his old pitiable sense of helplessness, and atones for a hundred other ills of city conditions. In his fraternal circle is the warmth and security which a man needs if he is not to succumb to the pressure of modern life. Little wonder is it that men so often think secretly of their lodge as "my mother" and cherish for it until death, a deep regard that no profane can ever comprehend!

What purposes were served by the Church in the Middle Ages? Have you experienced the loneliness of city life? Does moving about make for happiness? Why are so many families migratory? What are the effects on health, happiness, morality? What function is performed by the lodge in modern life? Have you found the lodge to be a circle of friendship? If not, why not?

In the ample framework of these facts one can see at a glance what Brotherly Aid really is. It is the substitution of the friend for the stranger. It is a spirit which throws round a man the comforts and securities of love. When "a worthy brother in distress" is helped it is not as a pauper, as in the necessarily cold fashion of public charity, but the kindly help which one neighbor is always so glad to lend to another. Masonic charity is strong, kindly, beautiful and tender, and not charity at all in the narrow grudging sense of the word. Nay, it does not wait until a brother is in distress but throws about him in his strength and prosperity the affectionate arm of friendship without which life is cold and harsh. Friendship, fraternity, fellowship - this is the soul of Freemasonry of which charity is but one gesture with a thousand meanings.

What is meant by, "Brotherly Aid"? How does your lodge assist a "worthy brother in distress"? Could you improve on the Masonic methods of charity? What is the difference between Masonic charity and public charity? What is the Bible's teaching concerning "charity"? (See I Cor. xiii.)

PART XVIII
SCHOOLS OF MASONIC PHILOSOPHY

LECTURES on the Philosophy of Freemasonry by Roscoe Pound, of the Law School of Harvard University, is the book wherewith to begin a study of the Philosophy of Masonry in a technical and systematic manner. The book is not bulky, and the language is simple, so that a novice need have no difficulties in reading it. I value this little manual so highly that I shall bring this series of studies of the *Teachings of Freemasonry* to conclusion by giving a rapid review of its contents, the same to be followed by reference to two or three schools not canvassed by Brother Pound, and by a suggestion of my own concerning Masonic philosophy.

The eighteenth century in England was a period of comparative quiet, despite the blow-up that came at the end of it, and men ceased very generally to quarrel over fundamental matters. It was a period of formalism when more attention was paid to manner than to matter. Also, and this is most important, it was everywhere believed that Knowledge is the greatest thing in the world and must therefore be the one aim of all endeavor.

William Preston was a true child of his century in these things, and he gave to Freemasonry a typical eighteenth century interpretation. This is especially seen in our second degree, most of which came from his hands, or at least took shape under his influence, for in that ceremony knowledge is made the great object of Masonic endeavor. The lectures consist of a series of courses in instruction in the arts and sciences after the fashion of school-room discourses. "For what does Masonry exist? What is the end and purpose of the order? Preston would answer: To diffuse light, that is, to spread knowledge among men." In criticizing this position Brother Pound has the following provocative words to say: "Preston of course was wrong in that knowledge is not the sole end of Masonry. But in another way Preston was right. Knowledge is one end - at least one proximate end - and it is not the least of those by which human perfection shall be attained. Preston's mistakes were the mistakes of his century - the mistake of faith in the finality of what was known to that era, and the mistake of regarding correct formal presentation as the one sound method of instruction. But what shall be said of the greater mistake we make today, when we go on reciting his lectures - shorn and abridged till they mean nothing to the hearer - and gravely presenting them as a system of Masonic knowledge? ... I hate to think that all initiative is gone from our Order and that no new Preston will arise to take up his conception of knowledge as an end of the Fraternity and present to the Masons of today the knowledge which they ought to possess."

Have you ever read *Philosophy of Freemasonry* by Brother Roscoe Pound? What can you tell about the eighteenth century in England? Tell what you know about William Preston. What was his idea of the purpose of Freemasonry? In what way was he wrong? In what way was he right?

Of a very different cast, both as to intellectual equipment and moral nature, was Karl Christian Friedrich Krause, born near Leipzig in 1781, the founder of the great school of Masonic thought of which Ahrens afterwards became so powerful an exponent. In the period in which Krause grew up conceptions of the human race and of human life underwent a profound change: thinkers abandoned their allegiance to the Roman Catholic theological leaders of the Middle Ages with their dependence on supernatural ideas and resumed the principal idea of the classical Greek and Roman scientists and jurists which was that man must be known for what he is actually found to be and dealt with accordingly. The goal of all endeavors, according to this modern way of thinking, is the betterment of human life in the interest of men and women themselves - a vastly different conception from that of the Middle Ages, which was that human life must be twisted and hewn to fit a scheme of things lying outside of human life. Krause believed that Freemasonry exists in order to help perfect the human race. Our Fraternity should work in cooperation with the other institutions, such as Government, School, Church, etc., all of which exist for the same purpose. According to what principles should Masonry be governed in seeking to attain this end? "Krause answers: Masonry has to deal with the internal conditions of life governed by reason. Hence its fundamental principles are measurement and restraint - measurement by reason and restraint by reason - and it teaches these as a means of achieving perfection."

Contemporaneous with Krause, but of a type strikingly different, was the Rev. George Oliver, whose teachings so universally influenced English and American Masonic thought a half century ago. Romanticism (understood as the technical name of a school of thought) was the center of his thinking, as religion was the center of his heart. Like Sam'l Taylor Coleridge, the most eloquent interpreter of Oliver's own period, he rebelled against the dry intellectualism of the eighteenth century in behalf of speculation and imagination; he insisted that reason make way for intuition and faith; he attached a very high value to tradition: and he was very eager to reconcile Christianity with philosophy.

"What then are Oliver's answers to the three fundamental questions of Masonic philosophy?

"1. What is the end of Masonry, for what does the institution exist? Oliver would answer, it is one in its end with religion and with science. Each of these are means through which we are brought into relation with the absolute. They are the means through which we know God and his works.

"2. How does Masonry seek to achieve its end? Oliver would answer by preserving, handing down and interpreting a tradition of immemorial antiquity, a pure tradition from the childhood of the race.

"3. What are the fundamental principles by which Masonry is governed in achieving its task? Oliver would say, the fundamental principles of Masonry are essentially the principles of religion as the basic principles of the moral world. But in Masonry they appear in a traditional form. Thus, for example, toleration in Masonry is a form of what in religion we call charity; universality in Masonry is a traditional form of what in religion we call love of one's neighbor."

Albert Pike was, during a large part of his life contemporaneous with Oliver and Krause, and consequently grew up in the same thought world, but for all that he worked out an interpretation of Masonry radically different from others. In spite of all his studies in antiquity and in forgotten philosophies and religions Pike, at the bottom of his mind, attacked the problems of Masonic thought as though no other man before him had ever heard of it. He was impatient of traditions, often scornful of other opinions, and as for the dogmas and shibboleths of the schools he would have nothing of them. What is genuinely real? that was the great question of his thinking: and accordingly his interpretation of Freemasonry took the form of a metaphysic. He was more interested in nature than in function.

"1. What is the end of Masonry? What is the purpose for which it exists? Pike would answer: The immediate end is the pursuit of light. But light means here attainment of the fundamental principle of the universe and bringing of ourselves into harmony, the ultimate unity which alone is real. Hence the ultimate end is to lead us to the Absolute - interpreted by our individual creed if we like but recognized as the final unity into which all things merge and with which in the end all things must accord. You will see here at once a purely philosophical version of what, with Oliver, was purely religious.

"2. What is the relation of Masonry to other human institutions and particularly to the state and to religion? He would answer it seeks to interpret them to us, to make them more vital for us, to make them more efficacious for their purposes by showing the ultimate reality of which they are manifestations. It teaches us that there is but one Absolute and that everything short of that Absolute is relative; is but a manifestation, so that creeds and dogmas, political or religious, are but interpretations. It teaches us to make our own interpretation for ourselves. It teaches us to save ourselves by finding for ourselves the ultimate principle by which we shall come to the real. In other words, it is the universal institution of which other spiritual, moral and social institutions are local and temporary phases.

"3. How does Masonry seek to reach these ends? He would say by a system of allegories and of symbols handed down from antiquity which we are to study and upon which we are to reflect until they reveal the light to each of us individually. Masonry preserves these symbols and acts out these allegories for us. But the responsibility of reaching the real through them is upon each of us. Each of us has the duty of using this wonderful heritage from antiquity for himself. Masonry in Pike's view does not offer us predigested food. It offers us a wholesome fare which we must digest for ourselves. But what a feast! It is nothing less than the whole history of human search for reality. And through it he conceives, through mastery of it, we shall master the universe."

Tell what you know of Kraus. What was Krause's conception of the purpose of Freemasonry? Do you agree with him? Tell what you know of Rev. George Oliver. What was his philosophy? What did he believe to be the purpose of Freemasonry? How would you criticize Oliver's theories? What was Albert Pike's general outlook? What is the end and goal of Masonry according to his theories? Do you agree with Pike's philosophy of Masonry?

Brother Pound, it seems to me, might well have included in his survey two other well defined schools, one of which, it is probable, is destined to out-do all its predecessors in influence. I refer to the Historical School, and to the Mystical School, neither of which thus far has developed a leader worthy of conferring his own name on his group, though it may be said that Robert Freke Gould and Arthur Edward Waite are typical representatives.

The fundamental tenet of the historical school is that Freemasonry interprets itself through its own history. This history is not broken into separate fragments but is continuous and progressive throughout so that the unfolding story of Masonry is a gradual revelation of the nature of Masonry. Would you know what Masonry actually is, apart from what in the theory of men it appears to be? read its history. Would you know what is the future of Masonry? trace out the tracks of its past development, and from them you can plot the curves of its future developments. Would you discover what are the ideals and possibilities of the Fraternity? study to learn what it has been trying to do in the past and is now trying to do.

This philosophy makes a profound appeal to men in this day when science, with its interest in history, development and evolution, rules in the fields of thought, and I have no doubt that more and more it will be found necessary for the leaders of contemporary Masonry to master the history of past Masonry, especially because Masonry, more than most institutions, derives from and is dependent on its own past. Nevertheless, in Masonry as in all other fields, philosophy cannot be made identical with history for the reason that such a method does not provide for new developments. What if some mighty leader - another Albert Pike, for example - were to arise now and give the course of Masonic evolution an entirely new twist, what could the historians do about it? Nothing. They would have no precedents to go by. An adequate philosophy must understand the nature of Masonry by insight and intuition as well as by history. Also, Masonry must not shut itself away from the creative genius of new leaders, else it petrify itself into immobile sterility, and condemn itself to the mere repetition of its own past. A great public institution must evermore work in the midst of the world and constantly learn to apply itself to its own new tasks as they arise in the world; otherwise it becomes no institution at all, but the plaything of a little coteric.

Of the school of Masonic Mysticism it is more difficult to speak, and this partly for the reason that mysticism itself, by virtue of its own inner nature, cannot become clearly articulate but must utter itself darkly by hints and symbols. On the one side mysticism is ever tending to become occultism; on the other side it has close affinities with theology. All three words - mysticism, occultism, and theology - are frequently used interchangeably in such wise as to cause great confusion of thought. Owing to this shuffling of use and meaning of its own ideas and terms the school of Masonic mysticism has thus far not been able to wrest itself free from entangling alliances in order to stand independently on its own feet as an authentic interpreter of the Great Teachings of the Craft. But in spite of all these handicaps a few of our scholars have been able to give us a tolerably consistent and, in some cases, a very noble account of Freemasonry in the terms of mysticism. Notable among these is Bro. A.E. Waite, whose volume, "Studies in Mysticism," is not as widely known as it should be.

To Brother Waite - unless I have sadly misread him, a thing not at all impossible, for he is not always easy to follow - the inner and living stuff of all religion consists of mysticism; and mysticism is a first-hand experience of things Divine, the classic examples of which are the great mystics among whom Plotinus, St. Francis, St. Theresa, Ruysbroeck, and St. Rose of Lima may be named as typical. According to the hypothesis the spiritual experience of these geniuses in religion gives us an authentic report of the Unseen and is as much to be relied on as any flesh-and-blood report of the Seen; but unfortunately the realities of the Unseen are ineffable, consequently they cannot be described to the ordinary non-mystical person at all except in the language of ritual and symbolism. It is at this point that Freemasonry comes in. According to the mystical theory our Order is an instituted form of mysticism in the ceremonies and symbols of which men may find, if they care to follow them, the roads that lead to a direct and first-hand experience of God.

What two schools of Masonic philosophy were omitted by Brother Pound? What is the principle theory of the historical school? Name some representatives of the historical school. What are some of the shortcomings of the historical philosophy of Freemasonry? What is meant by mysticism? How would you define Masonic mysticism? What is Brother Waite's theory of Masonry? Do you agree or disagree with him?

If I may come at last to speak for myself I believe that there is now shaping in our midst, and will some day come to the front, a Masonic philosophy that will not quarrel with these great schools but will at the same time replace them by a larger and more complete synthesis. I have no idea what this school will be called. It will be human, social, and pragmatic, and it will exist for use rather than show. It will not strive to carry the Masonic institution to some goal beyond and outside of humanity but will see in Freemasonry a wise and well-equipped means of enriching human life as it now is and in this present familiar world. We men do not exist to glorify the angels or to realize some superhuman scheme remote from us. Human life is an end in itself, and it is the first duty of men to live happily, freely, joyously. This is God's own purpose for us, and, unless all modern religious thinking has gone hopelessly astray, God's life and ours are so bound up together that His purposes and His will coincide with our own great human aims. When man is completely man God's will then be done.

As things are now, we men and women have not yet learned how to live happily with each other, and there is a great rarity of human charity under the sun. Why can't we learn to know ourselves and each other and our world in such a way as to organize ourselves together into a human family living happily together? That, it seems to me, should be the great object of Freemasonry.

More Masonic Books from Cornerstone

The Three Distinct Knocks
by Samuel Pritchard
6x9 Softcover 100 pages
ISBN 1613421826

Origin of the Royal Arch
by George Oliver
Softcover 202 pages
ISBN 1613420730

In His Own (w)Rite
by Michael R. Poll
6x9 Softcover 176 pages
Retail Price: $15.95
ISBN: 1-61342-017-X

Outline of the Rise and Progress of Freemasonry in Louisiana
by James B. Scot
Introduction by Alain Bernheim
Afterword by Michael R. Poll
8x10 Softcover 180 pages
ISBN 1-934935-31-X

Military Lodges: The Apron and the Sword
by Robert Freke Gould
6x9 Softcover 252 pages
ISBN 161342177X

The Master Workman or True Masonic Guide
by Henry C. Atwood
6x9 Softcover 396 pages
ISBN 1613420528

More Masonic Books from Cornerstone

Masonic Enlightenment
The Philosophy, History and Wisdom of Freemasonry
Edited by Michael R. Poll
6 x 9 Softcover 180 pages
ISBN 1-887560-75-0

Morgan: The Scandal That Shook Freemasonry
by Stephen Dafoe
Foreword by Arturo de Hoyos
6x9 Softcover 484 pages
ISBN 1-934935-54-9

Masonic Questions and Answers
by Paul M. Bessel
6 x 9 Softcover 144 pages
ISBN 1-887560-59-9

Our Stations and Places - Masonic Officer's Handbook
by Henry G. Meacham
Revised by Michael R. Poll
6 x 9 Softcover 164 pages
ISBN: 1-887560-63-7

Knights & Freemasons: The Birth of Modern Freemasonry
By Albert Pike & Albert Mackey
Edited by Michael R. Poll
Foreword by S. Brent Morris
6 x 9 Softcover 178 pages
ISBN 1-887560-66-1

Robert's Rules of Order: Masonic Edition
Revised by Michael R. Poll
6 x 9 Softcover 212 pages
ISBN 1-887560-07-6

More Masonic Books from Cornerstone

The Freemasons Key
A Study of Masonic Symbolism
Edited by Michael R. Poll
6 x 9 Softcover 244 pages
ISBN: 1-887560-97-1

The Ancient and Accepted Scottish Rite in Thirty-Three Degrees
by Robert B. Folger
Introduction by Michael R. Poll
ISBN: 1-934935-88-3

The Bonseigneur Rituals
Edited by Gerry L. Prinsen
Foreword by Michael R. Poll
8x10 Softcover 2 volumes 574 pages
ISBN 1-934935-34-4

A.E. Waite: Words From a Masonic Mystic
Edited by Michael R. Poll
Foreword by Joseph Fort Newton
6 x 9 Softcover 168 pages
ISBN: 1-887560-73-4

Freemasons and Rosicrucians - the Enlightened
by Manly P. Hall
Edited by Michael R. Poll
6 x 9 Softcover 152 pages
ISBN: 1-887560-58-0

Masonic Words and Phrases
Edited by Michael R. Poll
6 x 9 Softcover 116 pages
ISBN: 1-887560-11-4

More Masonic Books from Cornerstone

Historical Inquiry into the Origins of the Ancient and Accepted Scottish Rite
by James Foulhouze
Foreword by Michael R. Poll
6x9 Softcover 216 pages
ISBN 1-613420-26-9

A General History of Freemasonry
by Emmanuel Rebold
Translated by J. Fletcher Brennan
Softcover 434 pages
ISBN 1-934935-81-6

Lectures of the Ancient and Primitive Rite of Freemasonry
by John Yarker
6x9 Softcover 218 pages
ISBN 1-934935-10-7

The Schism Between the Scotch & York Rites
by Charles Laffon de Ladébat
6x9 Softcover 66 pages
ISBN 1-934935-33-6

The Ceremony of Initiation
by W.L. Wilmshurst
6x9 Softcover 74 pages
ISBN 1-934935-02-6

Museum and Memorial: Ten Years of Masonic Writings
by Mark A. Tabbert
6 x 9 Softcover 176 pages
ISBN 1-934935-83-2

10969779R00088

Printed in Great Britain
by Amazon.co.uk, Ltd.,
Marston Gate.